OUT & ABOUT IN LONDON

In association with London Transport

FRANCESCA COLLIN

WARD LOCK

A WARD LOCK BOOK
First published in the UK 1995 by Ward Lock
Wellington House, 125 Strand
LONDON WC2R 0BB

A Cassell Imprint
Volume © Ward Lock 1995
© Text Francesca Collin 1995
© Posters and advertisements London Transport Museum 1995

Distributed in the United States
by Sterling Publishing Co., Inc.
387 Park Avenue South, New York, NY 10016–8810

Distributed in Australia
by Capricorn Link (Australia) Pty Ltd
2/13 Carrington Road, Castle Hill NSW 2154

A British Library Cataloguing in Publication Data block for this
book may be obtained from the British Library
ISBN 0 7063 7374 X

Commissioning Editor Stuart Cooper
Project Editor Jane Birch
Designed by Richard Carr
Printed and bound in Spain by Cronion S.A.,

CONTENTS

❖

About London Transport

The Underground

With trains running every few minutes on most lines, the Underground provides a frequent and reliable service, 20 hours a day. Once you are armed with a copy of the Journey Planner (on the inside front cover of this book and also available free from ticket offices and Travel Information Centres), finding your way around the Tube is straightforward.

Tickets have to be purchased before you travel on the Tube, otherwise you are liable to a penalty fare of £10. Tickets can be purchased through ticket machines in the stations or from the station's booking office. Fares are based on a zonal system; further details are available from all ticket offices.

Most central London stations now have automatic exit and entry ticket gates. Put your ticket into the automatic gate, then take it out at the top, at which point the gate will open and you can walk through. If you have completed your journey the machine will keep the ticket, but valid season tickets or One-Day Travelcards will be returned by the machine on the automatic gate.

The Buses

London's famous buses now come in all shapes and sizes. Many are still red but other companies run buses in their own colours for London Transport. The London Transport Service symbol on the front of those buses that are not red tells you that Travelcards are accepted.

There are two types of bus stop: Compulsory (white background) and Request (red background). Buses will stop automatically to pick up at Compulsory stops unless the bus is full. Buses will only stop at Request stops if you signal to the bus driver by putting your arm out, or if you ring the bell while on the bus.

Night Buses

If you stay out late you can always get home by using one of the special night buses. These are identified by letter N before the number. Many of the night buses follow daytime routes, but others have their own routes. All night buses (except N31) pass through Trafalgar Square to the popular entertainment areas. But remember that One-Day Travelcards are not accepted on night buses and fares are higher than during the day. All bus stops become Request stops at night. Night bus maps and timetables are available from Travel Information Centres.

TRAVELCARDS AND SEASON TICKETS

You can purchase Travelcards valid for one or seven days, but these can be subject to early morning rush hour restrictions. Travelcards are accepted on all London Transport buses, Underground lines, Docklands Light Railway and most British Rail trains, within the zones you have paid for. Season tickets, which do not have rush hour restrictions, are valid for one week, one month or a year.

TRAVEL INFORMATION

London Transport Travel Information Centres (TICs) offer a wide range of services, including maps, phone cards, souvenirs and sightseeing tours. They can be found at:

BRITISH RAIL STATIONS

Euston
Victoria

BUS STATIONS

Hammersmith
West Croydon

HEATHROW AIRPORT TERMINALS

Terminal 1, 2 and 4 Arrivals

UNDERGROUND STATIONS

Heathrow 1, 2, 3
King's Cross
Liverpool Street
Oxford Circus
Piccadilly Circus
St James's Park

TRAVEL ENQUIRY SERVICE

Travelcheck is a 24-hour, recorded information service, available on 0171 222 1200. It is frequently updated and similar information is available on BBC Ceefax page 521, ITV Teletext page 194 and on display screens at TICs.

BRITISH RAIL

Those travelling from outside London can reach the city by rail and many of the services connect with the Underground network. While you are more dependent on timetables with rail, there are fewer stops so distances are covered more quickly. The main BR stations in London are: Charing Cross, Euston, King's Cross, Liverpool Street, Paddington, St Pancras, Victoria and Waterloo, which now gives you access to Europe through the Channel Tunnel.

INTRODUCTION

L OOK out of any window in London and what do you see? More than likely, your view will be of buildings, roads, traffic, perhaps a lonely tree. But if you look a little further, you will discover a side to the city that you may not have noticed before. This guidebook will help you to find a London you never imagined – a rural centre with hundreds of outdoor places to visit, things to do and wildlife to see.

Rural London may seem like a contradiction, but London is one of the greenest cities in the world, with over 170 square kilometres (67 square miles) of open space, ranging from the rolling landscape of Richmond Park and the historic ancient woodland of Epping Forest and Oxleas Wood to small, manicured triangles of grass round St Paul's Cathedral in the City.

Secret gardens have a special appeal for me and across London there are several places I discovered for the first time while researching this book which are now regular haunts. I have often been asked which is my favourite spot; the answer's difficult. I can visit the Chelsea Physic Garden and the garden at Fenton House over and over again, and still enjoy something new. But it is the Winter Gardens at Avery Hill in south London, a beautiful Victorian treasure trove of plants and birds housed in a musty old conservatory, that has become my favourite corner of outdoor London.

Outdoor London does not just mean the parks and gardens. There are over a dozen city farms and sixty or so wildlife reserves, not forgetting a handful or reservoirs, all of which provide an important natural haven for a diverse range of plants, birds and wildlife. I have included as many as possible in this guide, with directions to help you find the hidden spots and green secrets of London. The conservation and preservation of London's wildlife are crucial issues and many species have survived only thanks to the hard work of groups such as the London Wildlife Trust which strive to protect our environment for future generations.

Eating and drinking al fresco are fun, sociable ways to enjoy the outdoors. There are many good restaurants in London with tables outside, as well as plenty of pubs in scenic spots – along the river, for example, or hidden away in some of the Capital's prettiest corners. Alternatively, you can just buy some sandwiches and have an impromptu picnic in any of the open spaces described in this book.

Sport is a great way to get to know outdoor London, and has the added bonus that it'll keep you fit! I have included dozens of outdoor sports for all ages and interests, from favourites such as football, cricket and tennis, to archery, softball and swimming. Then, for the less energetic, why not try kite-flying on Parliament Hill?

London is a beautiful place once you know where to look, and you can do more than simply enjoy it; you can help to preserve its outdoor spaces for the future too. During research for this book, I discovered a fantastic variety of activities on offer and places to visit, all of which are covered here. I hope that this guidebook will enable you to see beyond the office buildings, traffic fumes and noise and to view London in a new light – as a city with a green heart.

Francesca Collin

Symbols used in this book

⊖	Underground station	⋙	River bus
BR	British Rail station	£	Small charge – less than £5
DLR	Docklands Light Railway station	££	Moderate charge – £5 and
❑	Buses		above
P	Parking available		
✿	Cycling permitted		

Overleaf: *Lincoln's Inn Fields*

❖

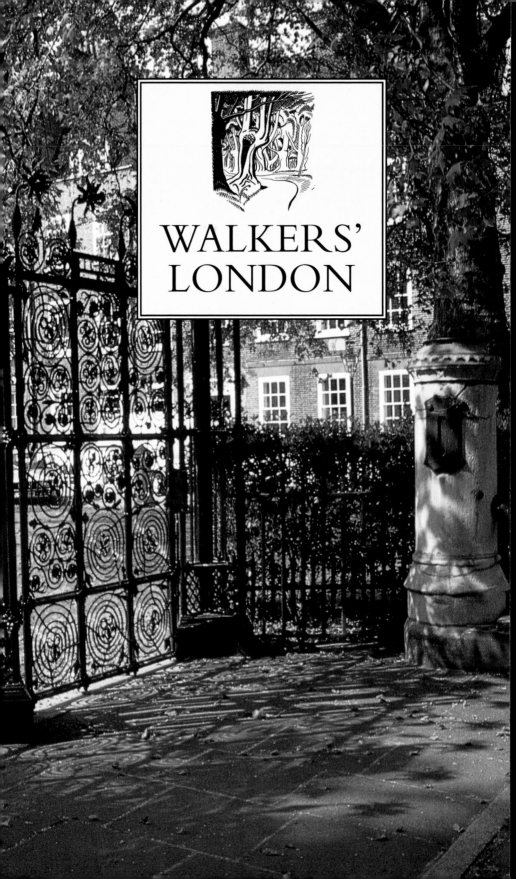

WALKERS' LONDON

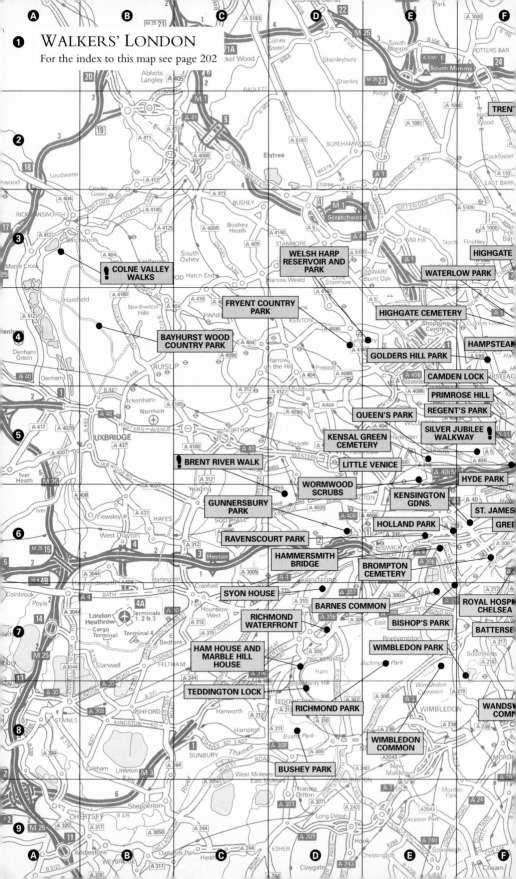

WALKERS' LONDON

For the index to this map see page 202

COLNE VALLEY WALKS

WELSH HARP RESERVOIR AND PARK

TREN

HIGHGATE

WATERLOW PARK

FRYENT COUNTRY PARK

HIGHGATE CEMETERY

BAYHURST WOOD COUNTRY PARK

GOLDERS HILL PARK

HAMPSTEA

CAMDEN LOCK

PRIMROSE HILL

QUEEN'S PARK

REGENT'S PARK

KENSAL GREEN CEMETERY

SILVER JUBILEE WALKWAY

BRENT RIVER WALK

LITTLE VENICE

HYDE PARK

WORMWOOD SCRUBS

KENSINGTON GDNS.

ST. JAMES

GUNNERSBURY PARK

HOLLAND PARK

GREE

RAVENSCOURT PARK

HAMMERSMITH BRIDGE

BROMPTON CEMETERY

ROYAL HOSP CHELSEA

SYON HOUSE

BARNES COMMON

RICHMOND WATERFRONT

BISHOP'S PARK

BATTERSE

HAM HOUSE AND MARBLE HILL HOUSE

WIMBLEDON PARK

WANDS COM

TEDDINGTON LOCK

RICHMOND PARK

WIMBLEDON COMMON

BUSHEY PARK

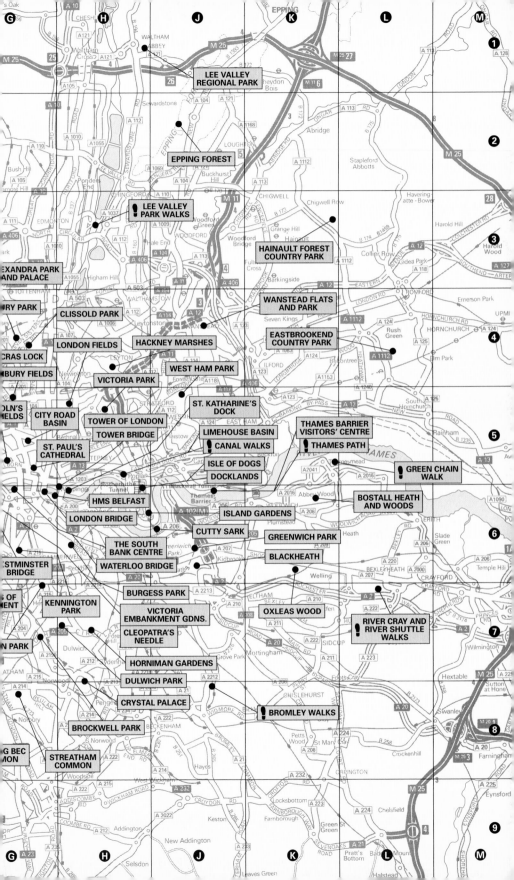

1
PUBLIC PARKS AND OPEN SPACES

L ONDON'S parks and open spaces are the city's greatest green asset. The numbers are impressive – 1,700 parks covering 170 square kilometres (67 square miles) – and they vary in shape and size from small squares of grass and manicured lawns to ancient commons and heathland.

This variety of parks is determined by their histories. In the centre of London are the royal parks, created by monarchs as royal gardens and hunting areas (see pages 45–54). Further afield are the commons, where people once grazed their animals. When landowners tried to enclose them in the nineteenth century, there was a public outcry and this led to the Metropolitan Commons Act of 1866, saving these open spaces for the public for ever. The appalling conditions in London's slums became an important issue at this time too, and the Victorians created numerous new parks to help improve the standard of living for London's poor. First came Victoria Park in the East End, shortly followed by Battersea Park and many more. Today, new parks are still being created, such as the John McDougall Park in Docklands and Burgess Park in south London.

HOW TO FIND YOUR PARK

Every park and open space has its own unique character and everyone will have their favourite. It would be impossible to list all 1,700, so I have chosen some 87 parks, squares and open spaces with the most to offer for the widest range of people. They are listed alphabetically by area and each entry has a brief description of the park's history and its main features. All parks are open from dawn to dusk unless otherwise specified, so times will vary considerably according to the season. The closest London Underground or British Rail station is given, together with information about buses. If you are travelling by car, you should find it easy to park in a nearby side street; if parks have parking facilities, these are mentioned.

CENTRAL LONDON

This section includes those parks in central London that are most accessible to visitors. The area covered extends from Regent's Park in the north to the River Thames in the south, from the City in the east to Chelsea in the west. For more information on royal parks in this area, see pages 45–51

❖

Brompton Cemetery

Old Brompton Road, SW7

The most famous 'resident' of this 16-hectare (39-acre) cemetery is Emmeline Pankhurst, leader of the women's suffrage movement, who also has a commemorative statue in the gardens outside the Houses of Parliament. In common with Kensal Green and Highgate cemeteries, Brompton Cemetery is a peaceful place in which to wander.

⊖ Earls Court, West Brompton

❑ C1, C3, 31, 74

City of London Parks

It was only when one third of the City was destroyed during the 1940–41 Blitz in the Second World War that space was suddenly available to bring flowers and trees into the Square Mile. Subsequent replanning and development mean there are now almost 200 gardens, churchyards and open spaces dotted all over this small area. Most of the gardens are quite small, ranging in size from a few square metres of raised flowerbeds on a street corner to the attractive modern landscaping of the Barbican Centre or the bowling greens of Finsbury Circus Garden, where you can watch pin-striped businessmen play at lunchtime!

Hyde Park and Kensington Gardens

See pages 45–8

Holland Park

Holland Park Road and Kensington High Street, Kensington W8

Holland Park is the most sophisticated, as well as the largest, of London's public parks. Linking a group of smart houses in Holland Park to the north with Kensington High Street to the south, the park was once the private grounds of Holland House. Today, the park still has the feel of a small country estate, with

Holland Park

beautiful formal gardens and peaceful grassy slopes leading on to wooded walks. There are also peacocks, ornamental birds, a mini zoo and a Rose Walk which ends with a statue of one of Holland House's former owners, Henry Fox.

For the culturally minded there is an open-air theatre (see also page 153), and for the hungry there is a modestly priced café, as well as an extremely good, but expensive, restaurant, the Belvedere (see page 171). For children there is an adventure playground and a One o'Clock club, and there are plenty of facilities for sport, including a cricket pitch and golf nets, football pitches, squash courts, a putting green and tennis courts.

⊖ High Street Kensington, Holland Park

❑ 9, 9A, 10, 27, 28, 49

One o'Clock clubs

Aimed at pre-school children, these clubs are run by local authorities in many parks. They are fully staffed and provide a range of activities, both inside the clubhouse, such as painting and looking at picture books, and outside, on swings and slides. Children must be accompanied by adults at all time, as these clubs are not a childminding service.

Lincoln's Inn Fields

Holborn, WC2

Lincoln's Inn Fields are one of the largest open spaces – 3 hectares (7 acres) – left in central London and are surrounded by elegant eighteenth-century buildings. They are always busy during the week – packed with office workers at lunchtime – but are a peaceful retreat at the weekend for a walk or to play tennis. The fields have always had a colourful history. They were originally common land known as

Ficetsfeld or Ficket's Field and a place notorious for beggars, side-shows and thieves.

The land was enclosed in the seventeenth century and almost lost to the public when Sir Charles Barry designed the new Law Courts. The land survived the pressure of developers and is a busy pedestrian thoroughfare, linking the surrounding law courts.

⊖ Holborn, Chancery Lane

❑ 1, 8, 25, 68, X68, 91, 168, 171, 188, 501, 505, 521

Regent's Park

See page 49

St James's Park

See page 50

❖

St Luke's Gardens

Sydney Street, Chelsea SW3

This park is a popular place to relax after shopping in the nearby King's Road. A hardplay area is available for five-a-side football, netball, volleyball and basketball. There are attractive flowerbeds, lawns and benches, as well as a few surviving gravestones from the churchyard of St Luke's, over which the park was built. Incidentally, Charles Dickens was married at this church in 1836.

⊖ South Kensington

❑ 11, 19, 22, 49, 211, 249, 319

Victoria Embankment Gardens

An attractive section of the river bank, the Victoria Embankment runs in two sections, either side of Hungerford Bridge. There is also a small area of gardens close to Temple underground station. The first person ever to suggest a river embankment was Sir Christopher Wren, in 1666, after the Fire of London. Work eventually began in 1864, despite opposition from commercial interests, such as wharf owners.

The total area reclaimed was 15 hectares (37¼ acres). The road was lined with plane trees and about 8 hectares (20 acres) were laid out as gardens.

Main Gardens

Villiers Street, WC2

The Victorian design of the main Villiers Street section was similar to today, with paths and a large number of flowerbeds. Deciduous trees were chosen, as it was thought that they were more likely to withstand smoke pollution.

Today, the flowerbeds remain, and the gardens are as popular as ever. In summer regular lunchtime concerts take place in the bandstand near the Villiers Street entrance – check park notices for details.

⊖ Charing Cross, Embankment

❑ 6, 9, 11, 13, 15, 23, 77A, 91, 176

Temple Gardens

Temple Place, WC2

To the east of Temple Underground station is a narrow strip of garden. In 1895 a bandstand was built which held concerts on weekday lunchtimes. Those attending included workers from the nearby printing houses in Fleet Street and the concerts were paid for by the newspaper companies. Today the bandstand has gone and the area comprises rosebeds and lawns.

⊖ Temple

❑ 1, 4, 6, 9, 11, 13, 15, 15B, X15, 23, 26, 68, X68, 76, 77A, 91, 168, 171, 171A, 176, 188, 501, 505, 521

Whitehall Section

Victoria Embankment, WC2

Of particular interest in this garden are the statues of military figures, such as Air-Marshal Lord Trenchard (1873–1956), founder of the Royal Air Force.

⊖ Charing Cross, Embankment

❑ 3, 11, 12, 24, 53, X53, 77A, 88, 109, 159

❖

Victoria Tower Gardens

Millbank, SW1

Just off Parliament Square, these gardens are a useful place to rest if you have been visiting the tourist sights around Westminster. They take their name from the Victoria Tower of the nearby Houses of Parliament and were laid out just before the First World War. There are some wonderful statues, including *The Burghers of Calais* by Auguste Rodin, which is a replica of the statue in Calais and commemorates the burghers surrendering to King Edward III in 1340 to prevent the town being destroyed by the British.

Θ Westminster

❏ 3, 11, 24, 77A, 88, 159, 211

LONDON'S SQUARES

Unlike many capital cities, much of London's centre developed without any overall planning and so missed out on the elegant tree-lined avenues of Paris and the geometrically arranged streets and parks of New York. Luckily, however, our forebears did leave us one important heirloom, the London square. From the 1630s onwards, when Francis Russell, 4th Earl of Bedford, commissioned Inigo Jones to lay out Covent Garden, squares quickly became important new features of central London's landscape which, by the eighteenth and nineteenth centuries, had spread into Belgravia, Knightsbridge, Chelsea and further afield.

There are over a dozen elegant squares dotted across central London, between Park Lane and Russell Square, and the most interesting are described below in alphabetical order. Sadly, several are open only to residents or key holders, but they are still worth viewing from the street, as they all contain attractive flowerbeds, lawns and trees.

Bedford Square

Bedford Square

WC1

Laid out in 1775, the square was originally part of the Bedford estate and was attached to the end of the Duke of Bedford's extensive gardens. His house was demolished in 1800, but the square was spared and is now the only complete surviving Georgian square in Bloomsbury. The oval garden boasts a fine selection of plane trees, but it is open only to residents.

ΘTottenham Court Road

❏ 1, 7, 8, 10, 14, 19, 22B, 24, 25, 29, 38, 55, 73, 98, 134, 176

Berkeley Square

W1

The inspiration for the song 'A Nightingale sang in Berkeley Square'

and the site of an annual ball, Berkeley Square, in the heart of Mayfair, has been one of London's most prestigious locations since it was first laid out in 1698. The square is named after Berkeley House, built in the middle of the seventeenth century for Lord John Berkeley of Stratton. It is open to the public and its tree-lined walkways are pleasant to stroll through, particularly in spring, when there is a glorious carpet of bluebells.

⊖ Green Park

❏ 8, 9, 14, 19, 22, 38

Bloomsbury Square

WC1

Founded by Thomas Wriothsley, 4th Earl of Southampton, in the 1660s, the square was the first of several to be built in this era. Today, although the square now covers an underground car park, its plane trees and seats have survived, and it still evokes the memory of the Bloomsbury Group of writers and artists of the early twentieth century who lived nearby.

⊖ Holborn

❏ 1, 8, 19, 22B, 25, 38, 55, 68, 91, 98, 168, 171, 188, 501, 505, 521

Gordon Square

WC1

Built by the architect Thomas Cubitt in 1850, this square was the heart of the Bloomsbury Group of writers and artists: Virginia Woolf, her sister Vanessa and Clive Bell, and the economist John Maynard Keynes all lived at number 46; Lytton Strachey was at number 51. The gardens are frequently used by London University students, but they are also open to the public between 8.00 a.m. and dusk daily.

⊖ Euston

❏ 10, 18, 30, 68, 73, 91, 168, 188

Grosvenor Square

W1

One of London's largest squares, Grosvenor Square is best known for its American associations. On the western side it is dominated by the impressive American Embassy and in the centre is a statue of President Franklin Delano Roosevelt. It is simple in design, comprising straight avenues of trees and walkways and is the largest square in Mayfair.

⊖ Bond Street

❏ 6, 7, 8, 10, 12, 13, 15, 16A, 23, 73, 94, 98, 113, 135, 137, 137A, 139, 159

Hanover Square

W1

A small and attractive square just off Oxford Street and Regent Street, this is a favourite lunchtime spot for nearby workers. Although there never seem to be enough benches to go round, there is plenty of grass to sit on instead.

⊖ Oxford Circus

❏ C2, 3, 6, 7, 8, 10, 12, 13, 15, 16A, 23, 25, 53, 55, 73, 88, 94, 98, 113, 135, 137, 137A, 139, 159, 176

Leicester Square

WC2

Now home to a wealth of cinemas and restaurants, and for many the centre of West End nightlife, Leicester Square is definitely not a place where you will find peace and quiet! The gardens have suffered as a result and the square is no more than a pedestrian precinct.

⊖ Leicester Square

❑ 14, 19, 24, 29, 38, 176

Manchester Square

W1

The main feature of Manchester Square, built in 1776, is Hertford House, the home of the Wallace Collection, a magnificent display of art treasures. The square is unfortunately not open to the public.

⊖ Marble Arch

❑ 2, 6, 7, 10, 12, 15, 16, 16A, 23, 30, 36, 73, 74, 82, 94, 98, 135, 137, 137A, 274

Chinatown
by Underground 中國城
nearest station Leicester Square

Chinatown
John Bellany ARA
one of a series commissioned
by London Underground

Red Lion Square

WC1

Just south of Bloomsbury, Red Lion Square, built in 1698, has been home to many famous writers and artists, such as Dante Gabriel Rossetti, William Morris and Edward Burne-Jones, who lived in number 17 between 1856 and 1859. The gardens, which are laid out as lawns and rosebeds, are open to the public.

⊖ Holborn

❑ 1, 8, 19, 22B, 25, 38, 55, 68, 91, 98, 168, 171, 188, 501, 505, 521

Russell Square

WC1

Russell Square derives its name from Lord William Russell, who married the daughter and heiress of the last Lord Southampton. The square was laid out in 1800 on ground previously known as Long Fields. Overlooked by the colourful terracotta bricks of the Russell Hotel, this square, one of the largest in London, is open to the public and regularly used by visitors to the British Museum. Although the square sadly lost many of its plane trees during the great storm of 1987, it still has its lawns and rosebeds and a pleasant café too.

⊖ Russell Square

❑ 68, 91, 168, 188

St James's Square

SW1

Set in the centre of one of London's smartest areas, this square was laid out by Henry Jermyn of St Albans, who leased 18 hectares (45 acres) of St James's Fields in 1662 and then bought the property a few years later. It quickly became a popular and prestigious address, although the square itself was somewhat neglected until the mid-eighteenth century, when it was finally paved and redesigned. Today it is still one of London's most attractive squares and it is open to the public from 10.00 a.m.–4.30 p.m., Monday to Friday.

⊖ Green Park, Piccadilly Circus

❑ 3, 6, 9, 12, 13, 14, 15, 19, 22, 23, 38, 53, 88, 94, 139, 159

Soho Square

W1

Soho Square was first laid out in the 1680s, in the centre of a cosmopolitan area which was then home to French Huguenot refugees. Today, the square is mostly used by dozens of people who work nearby who, on sunny days, fill up every inch of green space and eat their lunch.

⊖ Tottenham Court Road

❑ 1, 7, 8, 10, 14, 19, 22B, 24, 25, 29, 38, 55, 73, 98, 134, 176

OUTER LONDON

This section includes the major parks, commons, heaths, woodlands and open spaces throughout London, extending from Epping in the east to Kingston-upon-Thames in the west and Harrow in the north to Croydon in the south. For easy reference it is divided into north, south, east and west.

NORTH

Alexandra Park and Palace

Wood Green, N22

A popular venue for outdoor pop, jazz and classical concerts, this is one of the largest open spaces in north London, with fantastic views across the city from its highest points.

Alexandra Palace

A wide range of sporting activities is available here, including an artificial ski slope, football pitches, a cricket ground, playing fields, an ice rink and a pitch-and-putt golf course. Behind the palace (which is open as an exhibition and leisure centre) there is a boating lake. For children there are playgrounds and an animal enclosure.

Alexandra Palace is also near the end of the Parkland Walk, which runs from Finsbury Park, via Highgate and Queen's Wood to Muswell Hill (see page 80).

⊖ Finsbury Park, Wood Green

BR Alexandra Palace

❑ W3

P car parks

✪ cycling is allowed on the lower road

History of Alexandra Palace

The first Alexandra Palace, known as the People's Palace, was built between 1854 and 1873. Unfortunately, it burned to the ground only sixteen days after it was opened. The Alexandra Park Company did not lose enthusiasm, however, and proceeded to build another one, which was completed in 1875. By a stroke of bad luck, this one was destroyed by fire in July 1980 and has been replaced with a brand-new one which, fingers crossed, will not have the same bad luck.

The park has always had a colourful history, aside from all the fires. In the nineteenth century, it was used for some spectacular events and entertainment, such as horseracing and elaborate firework displays. The most famous display was called 'The Last Days of Pompeii' and took place in 1888. This elaborate and costly spectacle included a cast of 200 playing Roman citizens. The boating lake was decorated to represent the Bay of Naples, complete with temples, town centre settings and amphitheatres and the evening ended with an amazing firework display representing the eruption of Mount Vesuvius.

Clissold Park

Green Lanes, Stoke Newington, N16

See also page 107

Originally attached to a private home, Clissold Park has managed to retain many features of a small country estate, with acres of rolling parkland, home to a herd of fallow deer, and formal gardens.

Other features of the park are two ornamental lakes, an aviary and a small animal enclosure. For children there is also a playground, a paddling pool and a One o'Clock club. Sporting facilities include a bowling green, a football pitch, netball and tennis courts and a running track.

⊖ Manor House

❑ 106, 141, 171A

❖

Clissold Park

Clissold Park originally belonged to the Crawshay family and, in the late eighteenth century, the local parson, the Reverend Clissold, fell in love with one of the Crawshay daughters. Mr Crawshay forbade the young parson from visiting his daughter and their relationship seemed doomed. Happily, though, when Mr Crawshay died, the young couple were reunited, making the parson the new owner of Crawshay's Farm, which he promptly renamed Clissold's Place or Park – a happy ending to a romantic story.

Finsbury Park

Seven Sisters Road, N4

Before the park was laid out by the Victorians, this area had been a fashionable place for pigeon-shooting and tea-drinking in the eighteenth century. In the centre is an attractive boating lake, surrounded by sloping grassland and avenues of trees. There is also a nursery, a rose garden, a café and sporting facilities include tennis courts, a running track, and cricket and football pitches. It is also a popular venue for concerts and rallies.

The park is also the starting point for the Parkland Walk, a nature trail which follows a disused railway line up to Queen's and Highgate Woods (see page 80).

θ /BR Finsbury Park, Manor House

❑ W5, 29, 141, 171A, 253

P parking areas inside perimeter of park

✿ cycling is allowed on the central roadway

Fryent Country Park

Fryent Way, Kingsbury, NW9

Sandwiched between Wembley and Kingsbury, Fryent Country Park provides 120 hectares (300 acres) of woodland, hay meadows, open parkland, old ponds and hedgerows dating from medieval times. You can either explore the area alone or try one of the monthly guided walks given by Brent Countryside Rangers. If you would like to help in preserving and enhancing Fryent Country Park, the Friends of Fryent Country Park and Barn Hill Conservation Group, who run a wide variety of conservation projects, can be phoned on 0181 900 5038.

θ Wembley Park, Kingsbury

BR Kenton

❑ 79, 183, 204, 302, 304, 305

P car parks

Golders Hill Park

The Park, Golders Hill NW11

See also page 107

Although this park is only just down the road from Hampstead Heath, it has a completely different atmosphere. To the west is a short woodland garden walk which leads past tennis courts to Swan Pond, in the wilder end of the park, not

HAMPSTEAD HEATH

BY  TO

HAMPSTEAD OR
GOLDERS GREEN

far from the children's zoo. Among the park's other attractions is a walled garden, just north of the Lily Pond. Nearby too is a secret garden, simply known as The Hill. In 1775 this area was the subject of a riot when land was taken from the common by a Mrs Lessingham, who went on to build herself a house here, Heath Lodge. Ironically, history has turned full circle and now the surviving garden has been returned to the public. Facilities include a One o'Clock club, a miniature zoo, a café, a fenced-off toddlers' area and tennis courts. Brass band concerts are held. The entrance is just off Iverforth Close.

⊖ Golders Green

❏ 13, 28, 82, 139, 210, 245, 260, 268

Hampstead Heath

Hampstead, NW3

Hampstead Heath is probably the most famous open space in London and has a colourful history. It was a regular haunt of the highwayman Dick Turpin, while in 1763 Jackson, another highwayman, was hanged for highway murder behind the pub Jack Straw's Castle. It is not certain how Parliament Hill (excellent for kite-flying) earned its name: some believe that a Saxon Folk-Moot (an early version of Parliament) may have met there, while others claim that Guy Fawkes and his associates planned to watch Parliament burn from here. Today the Heath covers some 320 hectares (790 acres) of woodland and meadows, with splendid views of the city. It has not always been this large; from just 110 hectares (270 acres) in 1871, it acquired more and more land. Parliament Hill was added, along with Golders Hill Park (see above) and then Kenwood, the smaller Pitt House garden, the Elms garden and the Hill garden.

There are many miles of heathland, meadows, hills, woods and ponds to explore, and people need to come here regularly to get to know it really well. The most popular areas are around Kenwood House at the north end of the Heath, where on summer evenings you can sit and listen to wonderful open-air concerts (see page 155), and Parliament Hill, which gives a panoramic view across London. But it is worth getting off the beaten track to find other pretty, secluded corners too, such as Sandy Heath, across Spaniard's Road, the bathing ponds and

---

Literary Hampstead

Hampstead has been home to many important literary figures, including the Romantic poet Leigh Hunt (1784–1859). He moved to a small cottage in a hamlet known as the Vale of Health in 1816 and often wrote about its beauty in his poems. When his friend John Keats came to visit him, he was so taken by the area that he moved to Hampstead too.

Unfortunately Leigh Hunt's house has been pulled down, but Keats's house has been turned into a museum and is open to the public. (Wentworth Place, Keats Grove, London NW3, tel: 0171 435 2062.)

Open

Monday–Saturday, 10.00 a.m.–1.00 p.m. and 2.00 p.m.–6.00 p.m.

the Vale of Health at the western corner (once an eighteenth-century hamlet and now a collection of mansion blocks). There are several local groups concerned with the Heath which are worth joining if you live in the area. The oldest is the Heath and Old Hampstead Society, founded in 1897, which publishes a newsletter, holds meetings and organizes regular walks over the Heath. They can be contacted on 0171 722 9512.

For refreshment, there are cafés at Kenwood. For those interested in sport, there are an athletics track at Parliament Hill, bowling greens, cricket pitches, facilities for cross-country races and training, fishing on six ponds, football pitches, golf and putting, horse-riding (tel: 0181 348 9908), model boating, orienteering and swimming in the lido and bathing ponds (one ladies', one gentlemen's and one mixed) (see also pages 140–1) and tennis courts. For more details and to make bookings, phone the Sports and Entertainment Officer on 0181 348 9930.

⊖ Belsize Park, Hampstead
BR Hampstead Heath
❑ C2, H2, C11, C12, 24, 46, 168, 210, 214, 268
P East Heath Road car park, Parliament Hill Lido car park, Jack Straw's Castle car park and a few places in the west car park, off Hampstead Lane, near Kenwood House
✪ There are three cycle routes across the heath. One is the Hampstead Extension which follows Sandy Lane (from opposite Platt's Lane to North End). Note that you can only use this route before 10 a.m. The other two start from the car park on East Heath Road, passing just south of the general swimming pond. They then separate: one goes east to join Mill Lane, the other north to Hampstead Lane
Open: 24 hours (Heath only)

Highbury Fields

Highbury Corner, Islington, N1
Today, all that remains of Highbury Fields is a long, gentle stretch of grassland running from Highbury Barn in the north to Highbury Corner in the south, surrounded by some of Islington's most elegant Georgian houses. Just over a century ago, the Fields were part of a huge area of open dairy pasture which supplied milk for the city. Today, it is still an open space, but with the addition of a playground, swimming pool, tennis courts and football pitches.
⊖/**BR** Highbury & Islington
❑ 4, 19, 43, 236, 271, 279
✪ There is a route crossing north–south along the edge of the Fields
Open: 24 hours (Fields only)

Highgate Cemetery

Swain's Lane, Highgate, N6
Among the 45,000 graves in Highgate cemetery lie Charles Dickens's parents, his wife, his child Dora and several members of the gifted Rossetti family. The beautifully designed grounds of the west cemetery, which opened in 1839, set Highgate apart from the existing London cemeteries at Kensal Green and

Norwood, particularly the splendid Egyptian Avenue, the Cedar of Lebanon and the Terrace Catacombs. However, lack of control over the building of tombs and mausoleums, combined with the lack of proper maintenance of the site, meant the cemetery fell into disrepair and closed in 1975.

Luckily, through the hard work of the Friends of Highgate Cemetery, it has reopened, but because restoration work is still under way it is possible to visit the West Cemetery only by guided tour.

The east cemetery is open to the public every day, and although it is perhaps not as beautiful as the west cemetery, there are some interesting names to look out for – such as the writer George Eliot, the actor Sir Ralph Richardson, and the cemetery's most famous resident, Karl Marx.

⊖ Highgate

❑ C2, C11, C12, 143, 210, 214, 271

Open: Eastern cemetery Easter–end October, daily, 10.00 a.m.–5.00 p.m.; November–Easter, daily, 10.00 a.m.–4.00 p.m. (closed during funerals)

Western cemetery by guided tour only – phone for details on 0181 340 1834

£

Highgate Woods and Queen's Wood
Muswell Hill Road, Highgate, N6
Highgate Woods and Queen's Wood are such peaceful places it is sometimes hard to believe that they lie just a few yards away from busy roads. Originally part of the Old Forest of Middlesex, today Highgate Woods has an open landscape, while in Queen's Wood the trees and shrubs are denser. Although predominantly oak and hornbeam, many other species of tree now flourish here and small areas have been fenced off to encourage natural regeneration. Facilities include a café, a children's playground, as well as football and cricket pitches.

⊖ Highgate

❑ 43, X43, 134, 234, 263

Primrose Hill
Prince Albert Road, Primrose Hill, NW1
Primrose Hill lies to the north of Regent's Park, across Prince Albert Road, and is a wonderful place for kite-flying. From the top of the hill (64 metres/209 feet), the view is breathtaking too, so it is well worth the effort of walking up.

⊖ Chalk Farm

BR Primrose Hill

❑ C11, C12, 31, 274

Queen's Park

Harlist Road, Kilburn, NW6

In 16 hectares (30 acres), Queen's Park packs in a good range of activities for all interests, as well as plenty of open space to walk and enjoy. In the summer, special entertainments, such as parties, games and activity days, are laid on for children, and the paddling pool is open then too. There are also playgrounds which children can use all year round. Other facilities include a bandstand and, for sports enthusiasts, there are tennis courts and a pitch-and-putt golf course.

BR Brondesbury Park

❑ 206

Waterlow Park

Highgate High Street, Highgate, N6

A charming park centred on Lauderdale House, a Grade I listed building which was gutted by fire in 1963. Some of the building has been restored and it now houses a small art gallery and a restaurant – a nice place to stop for tea after visiting nearby Highgate Cemetery. Children have a play area and there are also tennis courts and a putting green.

⊖ Highgate

❑ 4, C11, C12, 143, 210, 271

Welsh Harp Reservoir and Park

Aboyne Road/Birchen Grove, Neasden, NW9

This 70-hectare (170-acre) stretch of countryside and water is flanked by the busy North Circular and Edgware Roads. The reservoir at Welsh Harp (also known as Brent Reservoir) is the centre of the Welsh Harp Sailing Association (see also page 142, while its shores offer a rich mixture of wetland and waterside habitats for plants, wildlife and birds. The Harp is particularly famous for its great crested grebe and there are over 140 bird species to be seen at different times of the year. With such a bounty of wildlife to be protect-ed and preserved, the Welsh Harp has been designated a Site of Special Scientific Interest (SSSI) and is proposed as a local nature reserve.

BR Wembley Park,

❑ 182, 245, 297, 302

P car parks

SOUTH

Bostall Heath and Woods, and Lesnes Abbey Woods

Knee Hill, Abbey Wood, SE2

The two greatest attractions of these adjoining open spaces are the ruins of the twelfth-century Lesnes Abbey and the 8 hectares (20 acres) of wild daffodils in the spring. Along with Bostall Heath and Woods, this is the largest area of woodland in south London. The terrain is rugged and varied and the area is also rich in fossils. Permission to dig or sift for fossils can be obtained only from the park manager. There is also a pond which provides a refuge for wildlife and a café for refreshment.

Sports facilities include a bowling green, cricket practice nets, a permanent orienteering course and a camping site (open all year; 0181 310 2233).

BR Abbey Woods

❑ B11, 99, 180, 272, 401, 469

Avery Hill Park

Avery Hill Road, Eltham, SE9

The magnificent domed Winter Garden with its splendid selection of exotic trees, flowers, ferns and fruit make this a fascinating botanic garden to visit (see page 109). But the rest of the park is worth exploring too, especially the walled rose garden.

A café provides refreshments, and there are children's playgrounds, playing fields and tennis courts.

BR Eltham Park, Falconwood

❑ 132, 228, 233, 328

Open: Monday–Sunday 10.00 a.m.–4.00 p.m. (closed 1.00 p.m.–2.00 p.m.)

Barnes Common and Putney Lower Common

Queens Ride, Barnes, SW13

Until the end of the nineteenth century Barnes Common was marshy. Today its abundance of lush vegetation and wildlife warrant its designation as a Site of Special Scientific Interest (SSSI). Putney Lower Common to the east is a mixture of shrub, flat grassland and meadow. Elder, hawthorn and oak add to the habitat, as do the mature trees of Putney cemetery, where you might catch a glimpse of a woodpecker. The most attractive part, though, is a riverside strip following the Beverley Brook, which provides a pleasant footpath between the two commons and the Thames.

This open site provides plenty of space for cricket and football pitches, a recreation ground, a running track, a bowling green and tennis courts.

⊖ East Putney, Putney Bridge

BR Putney

❑ 22, 33, R61, 72, 265

Battersea Park

Prince of Wales's Drive, Battersea, SW11

Battersea is the second park to have been specifically created for Londoners rather than royalty (the first is Victoria Park). It opened in 1858 and instantly became the centre of the Victorian craze for cycling. In 1951 Battersea Park was one of the main centres for the Festival of Britain. There are still vestiges of the Festival Gardens and the Fountains in the park; the rectangular lake, fountains and steps all formed part of 'The Great Vista'. Osbert Lancaster's fountains are flanked by two high colonnades by the artist John Piper and are the largest in London. The park is well known for its exotic trees, such as the tallest-known black walnut (34 metres, 110 feet), a strawberry, a Kentucky coffee and a foxglove tree, and you can follow a special tree trail, introducing all the different varieties. There are also a 1-hectare (2-acre) nature reserve, a herb garden and an Old English Garden,

constructed in 1912 on the site of a small botanic garden, all of which are worth exploring.

A more recent arrival is the magnificent peace pagoda at the north end of the park. Dedicated to the realization of universal peace, it was given to the park in 1985 by the Most Venerable Nichidatsu Fujii, of the Japanese Buddhist order Nipponzan Myohoji. Other points of interest include the deer enclosure, which is now also home to a community of wallabies, as well as a colourful collection of peacocks, cranes and guinea fowl, and the Victorian ornamental boating lake in the centre of the park.

Battersea is a wonderful park for children. One of its main attractions is a children's zoo: animals and birds include flamingos, mongooses, meerkats and boa constrictors (see also page 106). London's largest adventure playground is here and there is also a One o'Clock club.

Sports facilities include twenty-one tennis courts, an athletics track, a Trim Trail, a bowling green and all-weather sports pitches.

⊖ Sloane Square
BR Battersea Park, Queenstown Road
❑ 19, 44, 45A, 49, 137, 137A, 249, 319, 344
P car parks
✿ cycling is allowed on the roads in the park

Blackheath
Shooters Hill, Blackheath, SE3
Over the road from Greenwich Park is Blackheath, a vast treeless plain. Although this ancient heath is now visually bleak, it was once quite thickly wooded. Originating as common land, it has been the scene of many fascinating historical events and this gives it more character than some later, more decorative parks. There are several possible explanations for its name: some say it is so called because victims of the Black Death were buried here, others that it is named after the rich, dark soil. It may even be a combination of the two!

Today the heath is a perfect site for sport, and facilities include bowling greens, football and cricket pitches.
BR Blackheath
❑ 53, 54, 89, 108, 202, 306, 380

Brockwell Park
Dulwich Road and Norwood Road, Herne Hill, SE24
See also page 116
Brockwell Park was once the home of a wealthy industrialist and the park was opened to the public nearly 100 years ago. To the west of the park is an

Blackheath

Blackheath is forever linked with the name of Wat Tyler, leader of the Peasants' Revolt. With an army of over 10,000 peasants Wat Tyler, a blacksmith from Dartford in Kent, took Canterbury and then marched on London. The army assembled on Blackheath before heading off, on 13 June 1381, for the capital. Their grievance: the imposition of a poll tax.

Initially the Peasants' Revolt attracted considerable support, and the army, now numbering some 100,000, was able to take the Tower of London for a short time. As a result, King Richard II and his advisers went to meet Wat Tyler at Mile End, and the king made several concessions, including abolition of the poll tax.

However, at a further meeting in Smithfield, Tyler was murdered and the Peasants' Revolt was then crushed. Many peasants were executed and most of the concessions granted were revoked.

attractive chain of ornamental lakes and near the house there is a delightful walled garden, the Shakespearian Garden (see page 116). There is also a flower garden, an aviary and the remains of a topiary garden – a large yew arch still exists to mark this.

Children are well catered for, with a paddling pool and playground. Sports facilities include a bowling green, an open-air swimming pool, and netball and tennis courts.

Θ Brixton
BR Herne Hill
❑ 2, 3, 37, 68, 68A, 115, 196, 322
✪ cycling is allowed on the outer paths

Burgess Park

Albany Road, Peckham, SE5

Burgess Park began life as a small strip of land 6 hectares (15 acres) in size, known as Camberwell Open Space. From these origins in the 1940s, the park has grown into one of the largest in south London.

It includes a wealth of facilities for children and adults, with new developments all the time. One of the most original features is a multicultural garden, with plants from countries such as Africa and the West Indies.

You can also follow an attractive tree walk, which points out some of London's most exotic species, such as the Himalayan birch, the dawn redwood and the swamp cypress.

Other facilities include a lake, football pitches and tennis courts, a café and a children's playground.

Θ Elephant & Castle
❑ P3, 42

Crystal Palace

Anerley Road, Sydenham, SE20

The dinosaurs in this Victorian theme park are still a favourite with children. Not far behind in popularity are the fair, mini steam train and pony and trap. There is also a maze, still surrounded by the original ring of trees from the 1890s, and a concert bowl where Sunday evening concerts are given. The National Sports Centre is also in the park (see also page 126).

The park also includes a museum, café and bandstand, where concerts are regularly performed during the summer (see page 154). Sporting facilities include a cricket pitch and tennis courts and there are also facilities for orienteering, boating and fishing. Camping facilities are available all year around (0181 778 7155).

BR Crystal Palace
❑ 2, 3, 63, 122, 137A, 157, 202, 227, 249, 306, 322, 352, 358, 450
P car park

Dulwich Park

College Road, Dulwich Village, SE19

The beautiful displays of rhododendrons and azaleas are the most attractive feature of this park, which is also home to one of the widest ranges of tree species of any park in London (a leaflet available from the park manager's office provides a useful guide to the thirty-two species in the park). The azalea and rhododendron garden dates back to the 1890s and is situated at the eastern end of the park, near Roseberry Gate, and is at its best in May. The crocuses and daffodils in early April are well worth seeing too.

The land of Dulwich Park was presented as a free gift to the public by the governors of Dulwich College in 1885. Originally meadows and fields, it was remodelled by the Victorian park designers, with a tree-lined carriage drive and boating lake, before it was officially opened in 1890. Today, there are also two ecology areas and a series of new 'touch' maps for the blind and visually handicapped, situated at each of the park's entrances.

Sports facilities include bowling and putting greens, a cricket pitch and nets, and football pitches. There is also a boating lake, children's playground and café.

Near Dulwich are two other smaller parks – Belair Park off Gallery Road and Cox's Walk (starting at the junction of Lordship Lane and Dulwich Common) – which lead up to Sydenham Hill Wood.

BR North Dulwich, West Dulwich
❑ P4, 115
✪ cycling is allowed on the central roadway

Greenwich Park

See page 52

Horniman Gardens

London Road, Forest Hill, SE23

See also page 108

Variety is the keynote to this park and gardens, from the secluded water garden and large formal sunken garden at the southern end of the park, to the extensive views and miniature zoo near the Horniman Drive entrance. There are also three nature trails and one of London's finest anthropological museums. The museum was set up by Frederick John Horniman MP, a Victorian tea magnate and anthropology enthusiast, who donated the park and museum to the public in 1902. The magnificent Victorian conservatory once stood in the Horniman family home at Coombe Cliff in Croydon and was rebuilt here in 1989 by English Heritage. Today, it is regularly used for concerts and exhibitions. It has a café, a souvenir shop and the museum holds regular workshops for children and adults. There is also an aquarium within the grounds.

In 1973 a strip of railway land was added to the park, for which three walks have been designed – the Railway trail, the Dutch Barn trail and the shorter Coach House trail. Copies of the three guide leaflets are available from the park manager's office and from the Horniman Museum on 0181 699 2339.
BR Forest Hill
❏ P4, P13, 63, 176, 185, 312

Kennington Park
St Agnes Place, Kennington, SE1
The famous actor Charlie Chaplin was born and brought up just around the corner from here in Kennington Road, and the park provides a welcome breath of fresh air to this built-up area of south London. The park's main features include a Charlie Chaplin Handicapped Adventure Playground, a One o'Clock club and a dog-free supervised play area, and for sports there are tennis courts, a floodlit all-weather games pitch and grass pitches.
❸ Kennington, Oval
❏ 3, 109, 133, 159, 185, 335

Oxleas Wood, Castle Wood, Jackwood and Shepherdleas Wood
Accessible from Shooter's Hill and Rochester Way, Falconwood, SE18
These woodlands and heathlands form part of the Green Chain, a sweep of open spaces extending 24 kilometres (15 miles) from the Thames Barrier and Thamesmead through to Cator Park, New Beckenham. The oldest parts are Oxleas Wood and Shepherdleas Wood, which date back to the end of the last Ice Age. The woodland is designated as a Site of Special Scientific Interest (SSSI) and contains a rich mixture of trees, shrubs and plants. There is a pattern of paths crisscrossing the woods and at the western end is Severndroog Castle, an eighteenth-century folly, built for Sir William James of Eltham Park in 1784. The plaque above the entrance explains that the tower commemorates the conquest of the Castle of Severndroog on the coast of Malabar in 1755.
BR Eltham Park, Falconwood
❏ B16, 89

Ruskin Park
Denmark Hill, Camberwell, SE5
The bandstand and the old pond, which date from when this land was part of the private grounds of Dane House, are the central features of this large and pleasant park.

Ruskin Park has many claims to fame. It was named after John Ruskin, the famous nineteenth-century art critic, who lived nearby at Denmark Hill, and the sundial in the centre of the park marks the site where the composer Felix Mendelssohn lived and wrote some of his most important works. Music can still be heard today at concerts held in the bandstand.

Children's facilities include a play centre, a One o'Clock club, a fitted playground, a paddling pool, and a children's and parents' area. Sport is catered for with tennis courts, football pitches and a Redgra sports area.

BR Denmark Hill
❏ 40, 68, 68A, 176, 185, 484

Streatham Common, The Rookery and Norwood Grove
Streatham High Road, Streatham, SW16

Streatham Common is a large open space at the southern end of Streatham borough with an ornamental pond, flower gardens, a paddling pool and plenty of sports facilities. The Rookery is an attractive, formally landscaped area surrounded by the Common and contains a number of ornamental flower gardens. It used to be known as Streatham Wells, after the medicinal springs here, and you can still see the remains of one of the wells in the Old English Garden. The main feature of Norwood Grove is a listed nineteenth-century building, known locally as the White House.

Horse-riding is a popular pastime here, and there are also facilities for tennis, football, bowling and other ball games.

BR Streatham
❏ 50, 60, 109, 118, 137A, 249, 250

Tooting Bec Common
Tooting Bec Road, Bedford Hill and Garrard's Road, Tooting Bec, SW17

The 80 hectares (220 acres) of Tooting Common combine both parkland and ancient mixed woodland. The three main areas are Furzedown, Streatham and Bedford Hill Woods. Follow the nature trail to explore its rich variety of woodland plants and animals (including nuthatches and woodpeckers). The lake supports many fish, and a variety of waterfowl can be seen on both the lake and the smaller pond. There is a café nearby for refreshments.

Tooting Bec Lido, an open-air swimming pool (see page 142) and Tooting Bec athletics track, with its eight-lane all-weather surface, are the best-known sporting facilities here, but you will also find tennis courts, football pitches, a putting green, a fishing area (for members of the local angling club), a small horse-riding arena and a bridle path which runs the length of the common.

BR Streatham Hill
❏ G1, 57, 60, 109, 115, 118, 133, 159, 200, 249, 250, 319

Wandsworth Common
Trinity Road, SW17/Bolingbroke Grove, Wandsworth, SW11

Wandsworth Common dates back to the eleventh century, when it was part of the manor of Battersea and Wandsworth. Although the land was owned by the lord of the manor, local people had specific rights, which included cutting wood and shrubs, grazing animals and digging gravel. As London expanded during the eighteenth and nineteenth centuries, pressure to develop the common increased. Luckily, this was prevented, and today it stands as a wild oasis in south-west London. It is an important centre for wildlife and the common's Nature Study Centre is a good starting point for information (open Wednesday and Friday, 2.00 p.m.–4.00 p.m. and Sunday 1.00 p.m.–4.00 p.m.). The area known as the Scope

is probably the most interesting part of the common for wildlife; in 10 hectares (25 acres) between Trinity Road and Lyfor Road, there has been a deliberate policy of minimal management to create an ecologically rich area. Now a mixture of developing scrub and grasslands, the Scope has colourful wild flowers from spring to autumn and provides a home for many animals, birds and insects, including frogs, warblers and butterflies.

Children's facilities include the Lady Allen Handicapped Playground, a One o'Clock club, and other playgrounds. For sports enthusiasts there are tennis courts, cricket and football pitches, a bowling green, and a Trim Trail. There is also angling (a rod licence will be needed; a permit is usually available on site via a fishing club representative).

BR Wandsworth Common
❑ G1, 77, 115, 219, 249, 319
P parking areas

Wandsworth Park
Putney Bridge Road, Putney, SW15
Wandsworth Park runs alongside the River Thames, across the water from the gardens of the Hurlingham Club. It boasts avenues of tall trees and ornamental shrubberies, as well as tennis courts, a bowling green and football and cricket pitches. For children, there is a playground.
⊖ East Putney, Putney Bridge
❑ 220, 270

Wimbledon Common and Putney Heath
Wimbledon Park Side, Wimbledon, SW19
This combination of native woodland, grassland and heathland forms London's largest common. The most popular area is the open space to the south and east, where there is an interesting example of an Iron Age hillfort, known, rather misleadingly, as Caesar's Camp. To the west, near the car park, there is a rare

hollow-post windmill, which has been converted into a museum illustrating the story of windmills.

The wildlife is a rich and varied mix of meadows, oak woods, heather and wild flowers. There are also four ponds, football pitches, several riding arenas and three golf courses. For children there are various playgrounds, and there is also a café.

⊖ Southfields (for Putney Heath), Wimbledon
BR Wimbledon
❑ 14, 39, 72, 74, 85, 93, 265
✿ cycling is allowed on cycle routes between the common and Putney and Roehampton

Wimbledon Park
Home Park Road, Wimbledon, SW19
Next door to the grounds of the famous All England Lawn Tennis Club (see also page 193) is a pleasant park.

Half the land, including the lake, has been absorbed into the grounds of a golf course, leaving 18 hectares (45 acres) as a large public park, with amenities such as a playground and café, and sports facilities such as tennis courts, football pitches and a bowling green.

⊖ Southfields
BR Wimbledon Park
❑ 39, 156
P parking areas

Woolwich Common
Academy Road, Woolwich, SE18
Originally a much larger common extending into Charlton, Woolwich Common has been slowly encroached upon by the army since the eighteenth century. In 1774 the Royal Artillery started to take over the land when they built the Royal Artillery Barracks and in 1802 the common was purchased by the Board of Ordnance for use as a large drill ground.

Today the land is still controlled by the Ministry of Defence and access is restricted throughout.
BR Woolwich
❑ 89, 122, 161, 178, 386, 469

❖

Eastbrookend Country Park and Chase Nature Reserve

Dagenham Road, Romford, Essex RM7

A new country park, due to open to the public in 1995, Eastbrookend is an ambitious project aiming to provide an interesting and ecologically valuable park on the former gravel land. It will also have general leisure facilities, such as sports fields, a kick-about area and a visitors' centre.

The Chase is already open (see page 90) as a nature reserve and Eastbrookend will contain woodland, meadows, ponds and wetlands, specifically to attract wildlife.

⊖ Dagenham East
BR Romford
❏ 174

Epping Forest

Epping Conservation Centre
High Beech, Loughton, Essex

Only a short distance from the centre of London, Epping Forest is an extensive area of ancient woodland. The original Forest of Essex stretched from the River Lea to the sea and was brought under Forest Laws (laws regarding the setting up of areas to be used by the Crown as hunting areas) by William of Normandy. Initially, commoners were able to use the land too. However, over the centuries, large areas of Essex were cleared and enclosed to raise money for the Crown. The City of London Corporation finally took responsibility for the land at the end of the nineteenth century and still manages the forest.

Not all the area is wooded; there are also vast swathes of grassland, heathland ponds and even bogs. It is a wonderful place just to wander and to observe the varied plant and animal life. There is a con-servation centre which gives information on the forest and organizes courses and guided walks, and there is a woodland path for wheelchairs. You can also go on the 24-kilometre(15-mile) Epping Forest Centenary Walk, or at least some of it (see page 78)!

Queen Elizabeth's Hunting Lodge

In addition to the woods and grassland, there are many interesting places to visit. There are two listed buildings in the Forest – Queen Elizabeth's Hunting Lodge at Chingford and the Temple in Wanstead Park (see page 41). Sports facilities include an eighteen-hole golf course on part of Chingford Plain, sixty games pitches, two golf clubs and three cricket clubs. There are also bridleways, fishing areas and a model aircraft flying site. Camping is possible at High Beech, Loughton (0181 508 3749/1000).

⊖ Epping, Loughton, Snaresbrook, Theydon Bois

BR Chingford, Highams Park, Manor Park, Wanstead Park, Wood Street

❑ 500, 502

P̄ car parks

Car the south part of the forest is accessible from central London on the A104 and A11, and the B172 (from the east) and A121 (from the west) lead to the north part of the forest

❖

Hackney Marshes

Homerton Road, Leyton, E9
This ancient marshland was originally the site of a Roman stone causeway that formed part of the link between London and Essex. The marsh is now a small part of the extensive Lee Valley Park (see below) and includes children's playgrounds, football pitches and a putting green.
Θ Leyton
BR Hackney Wick
❑ W15, 22A, 48, 56, 236, 276, 308

Hainault Forest Country Park

Romford Road, Chigwell, Essex IG7
This 365-hectare (900-acre) country park lies on the outer edges of London and combines woodland, farmland, golf course, sports grounds and fishing lake. The main feature of the park is a large wood, part of the Forest of Hainault, which once belonged to the Abbey of Barking. Saved from total destruction at the end of the nineteenth century, the wood is full of ancient woodland species, such as crab apple and wild service. There is also plenty of open space to enjoy, with regular activities and walks organized by the park office (0181 500 7353).
Θ Hainault
❑ 150, 206, 247, 362, 511

Island Gardens

Saunders Ness Road, Isle of Dogs, E14
At the southern tip of the Isle of Dogs is a strip of public gardens with spectacular views across the River Thames to Greenwich. The gardens are also a terminus for the Docklands Light Railway (DLR), and are close to the entrance to the foot tunnel to Greenwich (the tunnel has a lift which is open Monday–Saturday, 8.30 a.m.–7.00 p.m. and Sunday 10.00 a.m.–5.30 p.m., with no service on 25 and 26 December; the tunnel is open 24 hours a day). (See also page 52.)
DLR Island Gardens
❑ D7, D8, P14

Lee Valley Regional Park

Lee Valley Countryside Centre, Abbey Farmhouse, Crooked Mile, Waltham Abbey, Essex EN9
The Lee Valley Park stretches north along 37 kilometres (23 miles) of the River Lea, from Stratford in east London to Ware in Hertfordshire. Opened in 1967, it was the first regional park in Britain to be created specifically as a centre for sporting and leisure activities and for nature conservation.

A good starting point is the Lee Valley Park Countryside Centre at Waltham Abbey. Here, a wealth of informative guides and booklets are available to help you get more out of your visit. There is also a fascinating exhibition on the development of the valley, from a peaceful backwater to a major industrial centre and its eventual return to a peaceful haven.

Within the 4,050 hectares (10,000 acres) of the park there are dozens of different activities to enjoy, from camping, orienteering, golf and angling to ice hockey, tennis and, of course, walking. Contact the centre for more information.

The waterways are an important aspect of the park too. Angling is the most popular pastime here (there are twenty angling clubs), followed closely by sailing and boating. The main watersports centre is at Chingford (0181 531 1129). See also page 144.

The park is a wonderful countryside and wildlife oasis, especially the further north you go. There are a number of bird and nature reserves, farms, country park areas and gardens, as well as vast tracts of woodland, meadow and open space to explore. You can follow one of the park's self-guided circular walks or just wander – either way there are plenty of places to stop and have a picnic. The centre also organizes regular countryside events, such as the Discovery festival for people with disabilities and the popular winter Birdwatch. Phone for up-to-date events lists on 01892 713838.

If you want to camp in Lee Valley Park, there are several official sites:

Lee Valley Campsite, Sewardstone Road, Chingford, Essex E4 7RA
Open from Easter to end of October. Suitable for caravans, tents and camper vans.

Lee Valley Caravan Park, Essex Road, Dobbs Weir, Hoddesdon, Hertfordshire EN11 0AS
A secluded 9-hectare (23-acre) park in a riverside setting, suitable for camping and caravanning (01992 462090).

Lee Valley Circle Circuit at Eastway Sports and Leisure Centre, Temple Mills Lane, Stratford, E15 2 EN
An eighty-pitch camp site in 16 hectares (40 acres) of parkland, where there is also a 1.6-kilometre (1-mile) cycle circuit. Visitors can also use the sports facilities at the Eastway Sports Centre nearby (0181 534 6085).

Lee Valley Leisure Centre, Picketts Lock Lane, Edmonton, N9 0AS
A 2.5-hectare (6-acre) site ideally located for easy access to London. Visitors can use sports facilities at Picketts Lock Leisure Centre (0181 345 6666).

BR Waltham Cross (for Lee Valley Park Countryside Centre)
❑ 505 (except Sunday)
Car close to junction 26 of the M25; also accessible from the A406 North Circular Road and the A10 Great Cambridge Road
P pay and display car park at the Countryside Centre
Open: Park most sites are open dawn–dusk daily. *Countryside Centre* summer, 10.00 a.m.–5.00 p.m. daily; winter, 10.30 a.m.–4.00 p.m., except Mondays
££ for some activities

London Fields
Martello Street, Hackney, E8
Reputedly one of the burial places of the victims of the Great Plague of 1665, these fields were part of Hackney's common lands until 1872. Today, they remain an important open space and are well endowed with mature London plane trees spread over an area of grassland and a network of paths. For children there is a playground and paddling pool, and sports facilities include tennis courts, football and rounders pitches, and cricket squares.
BR London Fields
❑ D6, 26, 48, 55, 106, 236, 253, 277
❂ there are two routes across the fields which are part of a larger cycle route between Hackney and Islington

Trent Park Country Park

Cockfosters Road, Enfield, Hertfordshire EN3

This is a popular country park with masses to enjoy – including a nature trail, ponds, public golf course and designated picnic areas – all set in 170 hectares (413 acres) of grassland, woodland and lakes. In the centre of the park is the campus of Middlesex University, which uses the eighteenth-century house there as the main college building. There is also a special trail for blind or partially sighted people; a tapping rail is provided from the main entrance on Cockfosters Road and Braille notices describe the scenery. Remember to bring some cash though, as there is a charge to use the car park.

⊖ Cockfosters, Oakwood

❑ 121, 298, 307

P car park (£)

Open: daily 7.30 a.m.–½ hr before sunset

Victoria Park

Old Ford Road and Grove Road, South Hackney, E9

Victoria Park was the first of London's parks to be created for the people rather than for royalty. It was opened and was laid out between 1842 and 1845 to the design of James Pennethorne, a protegé of John Nash. It was opened at a time when sanitary conditions and appalling air pollution had made the East End a breeding ground for disease and ill-health. The park lies at the junction of the Hertford Union and the Regent's Canal, linking this with Mile End Park to the south and the extensive Lee Valley Park to the east. The Victorian drinking fountain in the centre of the park stands as a tribute to its Victorian heritage. It was the personal gift of philanthropist Angela Georgina Burdett-Coutts, the first woman to be honoured with a life peerage through her own achievements and not those of her husband.

Victoria Park

Wanstead Flats

To the east of the fountain is a small lake with a wilderness island and the Old English Flower Garden, a lovely secluded spot in which to rest. There are also two cafés and an open-air theatre, while, for children, there is a One o'Clock club and a playground. Sporting facilities include football, hockey and cricket, netball and tennis courts, and putting and bowling greens.

⊖ Bethnal Green, Mile End
BR Cambridge Heath, Hackney Wick
❑ S2, 8, 277
✪ cycling is allowed everywhere

Wanstead Flats and Park

Blake Hall Road, Wanstead, E11
An impressive chain of lakes is the main feature of this park close to Ilford Golf Course, Wanstead Flats and the City of London and Manor Park cemeteries. The park is the remains of a largely eighteenth-century formal landscape park and the setting of Wanstead House. Acquired by the Corporation of London in 1882, the park was incorporated into Epping Forest. Due to its mix of woodland pasture, scrub and water, the park has a considerable natural history and in particular supports a wide range of birds, such as herons. During the season, fishing is available (for a fee). There are also sports grounds, tennis courts and a café.

Don't be alarmed if you come across a herd of cows wandering across the road near Wanstead Flats – this has been common land for centuries. Today, this open green space is mostly used for walking and riding, although a large area has been turned into a golf course and there are playing fields to be found on the western edge.

⊖ Wanstead
BR Forest Gate, Manor Park, Wanstead Park
❑ 58, 101, 104, 308, 551

West Ham Park

Portway, E7
The 3-hectare (7-acre) garden in the south-east corner of the park provides a splash of colour throughout the year, while the nursery grows the flowers and plants used in the park, Queen's Park and the City's public gardens too. There are playgrounds for children, while sports facilities include all-weather tennis courts, football pitches, cricket fields, a basketball court and a Trim Trail.

⊖ Plaistow, Upton Park
❑ 104, 238, 325

Trim Trails

These are fairly recent additions to many parks and offer a chance to get fit for free. The trails are simple assault courses, comprising a series of mostly solid, wooden fitness equipment, such as step-ups and parallel bars, along with information on how to use them.

❖

West Ham Park

Although West Ham Park is not as well known as other parks in the East End, such as Victoria Park, it is of particular interest as it offers a fascinating insight into how many London parks evolved, from private estates to parks for the public. West Ham Park stands on the site of a sixteenth-century estate, Rooke Hall. In the middle of the seventeenth century, the estate was purchased by Sir Robert Smyth, a barrister and Alderman of the City of London. It was sold by the family in 1762 to Dr John Fothergill, a physician, botanist and patron of science. He enlarged the estate and developed a large botanic garden, the predecessor of today's nursery.

In 1787 the estate passed to the Gurney family, who were well-known bankers, and was home to a famous member, Elizabeth Fry, the noted prison reformer. Eventually the family decided not to live there any more and wanted to sell it. To prevent the land from being turned into housing, as happened with many nineteenth-century estates, it was bought by the Corporation of London and opened as a park in 1874.

WEST

Bayhurst Wood Country Park and Ruislip Woods

Brakespear Road North, Harefield, Middlesex, UB9

Bayhurst is part of the Colne Valley Park. To the east, the wood is linked by footpaths through Mad Bess Park Wood, Copse Wood and Ruislip Common to Ruislip Lido and Park Wood, which together form an extensive stretch of public woodland and water covering some 300 hectares (760 acres).

The main feature of the park is an open-air woodland craft museum where you can pick up new skills such as basket-making and weaving at the special crafts demonstrations (by prior arrangement only). There are also plenty of picnic sites, bridleways and nature trails to explore (details from the information centre). There's a café too (open in summer only). See page 77 for details on Colne Valley's self-guided walks.

You can contact the Park Office on 01895 630075 or phone Hillingdon Leisure Services on 01895 50111, ext. 2450 for further information.

⊖ Ruislip

❏ H13, 331

P parking areas

Bishop's Park and Fulham Palace Gardens

Fulham Palace Road, Fulham, SW6

Bishop's Park runs alongside the River Thames, just west of Putney Bridge. Its main feature is Fulham Palace, the former summer home of the Bishops of London and now an interesting museum with a wonderful garden (see page 110). On your way out you could take a look at the garden centre near the main entrance if you feel inspired after your visit!

The rest of the park comprises tennis courts and a putting green for sports enthusiasts, while for children there are paddling pools, a sandpit and playgrounds, including a special playground run by HAPA, the Handicapped Adventure Playground Association (0171 731 2753). There are also a boating lake and refreshment areas.

⊖ Putney Bridge
❑ C4, 14, 22, 39, 74, 85, 93, 220, 265, 270
P parking areas

Gunnersbury Park

Popes Lane, Ealing, W5
The park was saved from being turned into an airport in 1923, when the Civil Aviation Board decided it would be suitable for an airstrip as it was so close to the centre of London. There was a massive outcry, and by 1925 campaigners were able to save the land, helped in part by the financial aid of the Rothschild family. Today, the house is a local history museum which also has touring exhibitions and the park, although not exactly the most peaceful – lying near to the M4 and directly on the Heathrow flight path – is an excellent large space with ornamental lakes and plenty to enjoy. There is a café, and a children's playground. Sporting facilities include thirty-six football pitches, two miniature golf courses, two bowling greens, two putting courses and a riding school. Provision is also made for tennis, netball, rugby, lacrosse, cricket and hockey.

⊖ Acton Town
BR Gunnersbury
❑ E3, 7, 65

Kensal Green Cemetery

Harrow Road, Kensal Green, W10
Kensal Green was the first of the great commercial cemeteries of London and was set up in 1832 as an answer to the overcrowded and smelly existing churchyards. There are many famous tombs here, including those of the writers William Thackeray and Anthony Trollope, of Isambard Kingdom Brunel, famous for the Clifton Suspension Bridge, and Emile Blondin, the tightrope walker. It is also the resting place of 'James' Barry (1788–1865), Inspector General of the Army Medical Department who, on death, was found to be a woman!

⊖/**BR** Kensal Green
❑ 18, 23, 52, 70, 295, 302
Open: Monday–Saturday 9.00 a.m.–5.30 p.m., Sunday 10.00 a.m.–5.00 p.m. and bank holidays 10.00 a.m.–1.00 p.m.

❖

Ravenscourt Park

Ravenscourt Road, Hammersmith, W6

Once the estate of Ravenscourt House, the park has maintained much of the garden's original elegance. There is a scented Old English Garden in the north-eastern corner, specially created for the visually handicapped, and a well-designed curving bed of shrubs and trees shielding the park from the noise of nearby roads and railways. Other amenities include a café in converted stables and a summer theatre. For children there are a playground, a paddling pool, an adventure playground and a One o'Clock club. Sports facilities include a bowling green (dating back to *circa* 1750), tennis courts and football pitches.

⊖ Ravenscourt Park

❏ 27, H91, 94, 190, 237, 266, 267, 290, 391

Richmond Park

See pages 53–4

Wormwood Scrubs

Scrubs Lane, North Kensington, W10

The Scrubs is one of London's main sporting centres, with its West London Stadium and other facilities, including cricket pitches, tennis courts and a bowling green. The other notable feature is its size – 77 hectares (191 acres) – and, despite its proximity to the nearby prison and industrial sites, it is a colourful and cheerful place. For children there is a playground, and there is also a café.

⊖ East Acton

❏ 7, 70, 72, 220, 283

2
ROYAL PARKS

HISTORY OF LONDON'S ROYAL PARKS

THE central London royal parks (Hyde Park, Green Park, St. James's Park and Kensington Gardens) were originally acquired by Henry VIII in the early sixteenth century for use as hunting grounds. At the time the land was a mixture of rough pasture, woodland and marshes. The king enclosed the land and stocked it with game. Over the years the surrounding land was gradually developed and the parks became fragmented.

Situated in the heart of the city, London's royal parks provide a welcome breath of fresh air and a chance to escape from the fumes, the shops and the offices.

HOW TO FIND YOUR PARK

The royal parks in central and outer London are listed below in alphabetic order. All are open from dawn to dusk, unless otherwise indicated, and entry is free.

Driving is permitted only in certain parks – Richmond Park, Hyde Park and Regent's Park, where the speed limit is 24 kilometres (15 miles) per hour.

CENTRAL LONDON

Green Park
The Mall, Piccadilly, SW1
Over the road from St James's Park, Green Park lives up to its name. An expanse of grass and trees, this park is popular with softball fanatics on summer's evenings and is a popular short cut from Piccadilly to the Mall for pedestrians.

Although it is a small park and plainer than its neighbour St James's Park, Green Park's sloping lawns are a peaceful and pleasant place to rest.
Θ Green Park, Charing Cross
❑ 8, 9, 14, 19, 22, 38
Open: 24 hours

Hyde Park
Bayswater Road, Knightsbridge and Park Lane, W1
Lying in the heart of the city, this is probably the best-known park in London. The crown first took over the land from the abbot and convent of Westminster in 1536 – one of the rewards of the Dissolution of the Monasteries. Henry VIII preserved it as a forest for his private hunting, but it was later opened to the public by James I in the early seventeenth century. He was also responsible for creating the Ring, a fashionable carriage drive in the seventeenth and eighteenth centuries.

Rotten Row 1895   A.K.Zinkeisen

The land was never formally designed and has evolved in response to need. It was fortified during the Civil War (1649–58) and in the seventeenth and eighteenth centuries was used regularly for troop reviews on what became known as the Parade Ground. It still has its military uses today for gun salutes and inspections, and Guards from the Life Guards and the Blues and Royals pass through daily on horseback on their way to Horseguards in Whitehall.

The park has traditionally been a hive of activity. The first football games, known as 'Hurling Matches', were played here in the 1700s and it was here too that Joseph Paxton built Crystal Palace for the Great Exhibition of 1851. Marble Arch (just outside the north-eastern entrance) was once the site of Tyburn tree, a site of public hangings from 1196–1783. Speaker's Corner, in the north east of the park is worth visiting too. Go on a Sunday and listen to the soapbox orators. Anyone can go and speak, provided they keep within the bounds of obscenity and do not disturb the peace.

Hyde Park is a park to enjoy. It is often used for rallies, open-air concerts, fun runs and fireworks displays, as well as by joggers, sunbathers and those who just want a pleasant stroll.

If you're in need of refreshment, there are several kiosks dotted about the park, as well as the Dell Restaurant, which is situated at the Hyde Park Corner end of the Serpentine (open daily 9.00 a.m.–6.00 p.m. during the height of the season and 9.00 a.m.–5.30 p.m. for the rest of the year).

Sports facilities abound here. There are four hard tennis courts which can be booked up to two full days in advance, in person only (sessions one hour long; open 8.00 a.m.–1 hour before sunset daily). Table tennis is played on the south bank of the Serpentine near the Lido.

The Serpentine Lido is a centre of activity too. Swimming is possible between May and the end of September between 10.00 a.m. and 6.00 p.m. Water in the lido is fully chlorinated for safe swimming and life-guards are always on duty. Boating is possible too: rowing boats, paddle boats and canoes can be hired from the boathouse situated on the north side of the Serpentine from March to October (0171 262 3751).

Hyde Park is the only open place in central London where horseriding by members of the public is allowed. For more information on riding schools, see page 138. Casual bowling is possible on the bowling green in the west corner of Hyde Park (May–September, 12.00 a.m.–1 hour before sunset). Putting takes place near the bowling green (May–September, 8.00 a.m.–1 hour before sunset).

⊖ Hyde Park Corner, Knightsbridge, Lancaster Gate, Marble Arch

❑ C1, 2, 6, 7, 9, 10, 12, 14, 15, 16, 16A, 19, 22, 23, 30, 36, 38, 52, 73, 74, 82, 94, 98, 135, 137, 137A, 274

P two free car parks in the centre of the park next to the Serpentine; some free parking spaces along the road linking Alexandra Gate in Kensington and Victoria Gate in Bayswater

✿ there are cycle routes crossing the park north to south, parallel to Park Lane, and along both sides of the Serpentine

Open: 6.00 a.m.–12.00 p.m. daily

Kensington Gardens

Bayswater Road and Kensington Gore, Kensington, W8

Over the road from Hyde Park, but with a totally different atmosphere, are Kensington Gardens. Originally, this land was part of the hunting grounds of

Hyde Park

Hyde Park, but in 1689 William III moved to what was then a wealthy merchant's house, Nottingham House, and created Kensington Palace. Initially only a limited amount of ground was laid out to the south and north of the palace, but this was later extended, and in 1728 a formal design by Charles Bridgeman was implemented which created a series of major avenues radiating from the palace.

This layout, although blurred, is still visible and in recent years much has been done to restore and replant the avenues. The gardens are dominated by the formal avenues and dappled parkland glades between them. The other major features date from the Victorian period. Queen Victoria was born in Kensington Palace and it was here that she held her first meeting with her ministers as queen. Disturbed by the run-down state of the gardens, she and Prince Albert set about providing facilities for the public. When Albert died she erected a memorial to him at the Queens Gate entrance to the gardens which, together with the Albert Hall over the road, dominates the area to the south.

Queen Victoria laid down strict dress codes for people visiting Kensington Gardens, but naturally these do not apply today. However, the gardens do have a more exclusive atmosphere than Hyde Park, possibly because Kensington Palace is still a royal residence. Some of the palace gardens are open to the public and they are worth walking through. The sunken garden is especially attractive and the orangery is a lovely cool place to stop on a hot day, with its shading plants, benches and statues.

The gardens are a wonderful place for children to explore. To the north is the Dogs' Cemetery, founded by the Duke of Cambridge in 1880 for one of his wife's pets. There is also a children's playground nearby and the stump of an oak tree, known as Elfin Oak, full of carved wooden gnomes, fairies and little animals. The oak was first placed here in 1930 and has recently been restored by the comic actor Spike Milligan. In the centre of the park is the Round Pond, ideal for model sailing boats, and also George Frederick Watt's statue of Physical Energy, a rider on a horse. To the west is the statue of Peter Pan with his fairy entourage, not forgetting the more sophisticated sculpture, *The Arch*, by Henry Moore over the Serpentine.

⊖ High Street Kensington, Knightsbridge
❑ 9, 10, 12, 49, 52, 70, 94
P in Hyde Park parking areas
✪ on cycle routes which run north–south and on road running east–west in front of the Albert Memorial

Regent's Park

Off Prince Albert Road, Albany Street,
Marylebone Road and Park Road,
Marylebone, NW1

Unlike the other royal parks, Regent's Park was developed specifically as a speculative property venture. As with the others, it had its origins as hunting grounds and then farmland, but in the early nineteenth century John Nash conceived the idea for George IV of building fifty villas in classical style within a private landscaped part, and so the park was laid out in its present form between 1812 and 1827 by John Nash and opened in 1838. Although the landscaped park was created as a series of lawns with plantations to lead to vistas and large areas of water, the plans for the villas were never fully realized and only two remain. Nash's plan was to have the canal running right through the centre of the park but there were so many objections that he had to reroute it along the northern edge. (See also page 57).

In 1830 a botanic garden was developed in the centre of the park and this in turn gave way to Queen Mary's Garden in 1932. Today it houses an extensive collection of both modern and old roses (see also page 112). In the outer park are the famous Nesfield Gardens, packed with brilliantly coloured flowers almost all year round.

Queen Mary's Garden

London Zoo is one of the main attractions of this park (see page 105). In the summer, there is also open-air theatre in the centre of the park – check the newspapers and listings magazines for times and dates.

One of the best sports facilities is the Regent's Park Golf School (see page 129).

⊖ Baker Street, Camden Town, Great Portland Street, Regent's Park
BR Primrose Hill

❑ C2, 13, 18, 24, 27, 29, 30, 31, 82, 113, 134, 135, 139, 168, 214, 253, 274

P two car parks in Regent's Park, one near the Zoo, the other near Gloucester Gate. Meter parking spaces are available along the Outer Circle at the following times: Monday–Friday 9.00 a.m.–6.00 p.m.; Saturday 9.00 a.m. – 1.00 p.m. Parking is free on Saturday afternoon and all day Sunday

✪ allowed only on the Inner and Outer Circles

St James's Park

The Mall, Horse Guards Road, Birdcage Walk, St James's, SW1
The formality of St James's Park is in total contrast to the openness of the neighbouring Green Park (see page 45). Some of the city's most popular tourist attractions, such as Buckingham Palace and Whitehall, overlook this park, and the constant ebb and flow of visitors makes it difficult to forget you are in the city centre. All the same, St James's Park is a perfect place to collapse into a deckchair and recover from the hurly-burly of the West End.

Henry VIII acquired St James's Park in the early part of the sixteenth century when it was a leper colony and turned the marshy land into a game reserve. St James's Palace was built and other government buildings and residences grew up around the boundary of the park. During the reign of Charles I the park was laid out in the French style with a formal canal, but in 1842 John Nash remodelled the gardens into its current informal English style.

St James's Park

Birds have always played an important role in the park. King James I was a keen ornithologist, as was King Charles (who developed aviaries), and his hobby gave rise to the name of the adjacent road, Birdcage Walk. During his reign a pair of pelicans was donated to the collection and a birdkeeper was appointed – a post which continues today, as does the presence of the famous pelicans. The park's lake is also home to many other waterbirds, from Canada geese and black swans to the less well-known Baham pintail and chiloe wigeon.

One of the greatest pleasures of St James's Park is to lie back in a deckchair and listen to a performance by the Royal Parks Band. Concerts are held throughout the summer months from early afternoon to mid-evening (see page 154). Be warned, though: you will have to pay a small charge to use a deckchair, but it is worth the price.

⊖ Green Park, St James's

❑ 8, 9, 11, 14, 19, 22, 24, 38, 211, 507

OUTER LONDON

Bushy Park and Hampton Court Palace and Gardens

Sandy Lane, Middlesex TW11 and Hampton Court Road, Middlesex TW8
See also page 110

Bushy Park was created by Henry VIII as an extension of Hampton Court in the 1530s. Originally less than 80 hectares (200 acres), it now covers over 400 hectares (1,000 acres) of open grassland, which seem all the more spacious after the formality of Hampton Court Palace Gardens. The main features are the glorious Chestnut Avenue, created by Sir Christopher Wren, which runs through the centre of the park and the herds of beautiful fallow, roe and red deer which roam freely. As with Richmond, continuous use as a deer park has made the landscape rich in wildlife.

There are a number of plantations fenced off to protect them from the deer and one of these, the Woodland Garden, is a delightful shady oasis through which a number of streams meander. These streams were created by diverting water from the Longford river, an artificial watercourse developed in the late seventeenth century to supply water from the nearby River Colne to the fountains at Hampton Court Palace. At the same time, Francesco Fanelli was commissioned to design the Diana fountain, which was originally sited in the Privy Garden at Hampton Court, but was moved to the pool at the south of Chestnut Avenue at the end of the seventeenth century. The ponds and small lakes within the park were originally needed for drinking water for the deer and other livestock, but they are now used for fishing, sailing model boats and as a home for waterfowl.

Although Hampton Court Palace and Garden are not royal parks (although, confusingly, they are Crown estate), they are worth describing here as they lie just over the road from Bushy Park. In 1514 Cardinal Wolsey ordered building to begin on Hampton Court Palace and in 1525 he presented it to King Henry VIII in a vain attempt to retain his favour. The Palace today bears the distinct and varied mark of almost five centuries of royal history. The garden's most popular features are the famous maze, which is great fun to get lost in, and the Great Vine, which is over 200 years old.

The overall layout dates from Henry VIII's time but only a small part, the Knot Garden, renovated in 1927, bears any resemblance to how it originally looked. In 1662 Charles II ordered the digging of a great canal, the Long Water, along the east front. This influenced the design of William and Mary's gardens, with their three great avenues of yew trees. The Privy Garden on the south (recently restored) was originally William III's private garden. The maze was planted in the 1690s and is now the only remaining part of the wilderness areas of the garden. Nearby are the tiltyards, which were built by Henry VIII for jousting tournaments and now house two restaurants.

BR Hampton Wick

❑ R68, 111, 267, 411, 726

〰️ boat from Westminster, Charing Cross, Richmond or Kingston

Ⓟ Bushy Park (free) or Hampton Court car park (££)

✪ cycle routes in Bushy Park; no cycling at all in Hampton Court Palace Gardens

Open: mid-March–mid-October, 9.30 a.m.–6.00 p.m., except Mondays, 10.15 a.m.–6.00 p.m.; mid-October–mid-March, 9.30 a.m.–4.30 p.m., except Mondays, 10.15 a.m.–4.30 p.m.

Free entry to parks but there is a charge (££) for entry to Hampton Court Palace, the Real Tennis Courts and the maze

Greenwich Park
Romney Road, Charlton Way, Greenwich, SE10
Greenwich Park now tends to be associated with the Maritime Museum and the Royal Observatory, but it was originally created by Henry VI in 1433 as a deer park. It has always had close links with royalty, especially Queen Elizabeth I, who loved to stay at Greenwich Palace; it was only in 1992 that an oak tree reputedly planted during her reign finally succumbed to old age and had to be removed. Greenwich Palace was pulled down by Charles II in 1675 and never replaced, although other notable buildings in the park still stand. There is Christopher Wren's Royal Observatory, through the courtyard of which runs the Prime Meridian Line – with a foot on either side, you stand in both the eastern and the western hemispheres. Inigo Jones's Queen's House, built for Queen Anne of Denmark, wife of James I, is also worth a visit.

From the statue of General Wolfe, the British general who took Quebec, at the top of the park (48 metres/155 feet above the Thames) there is a wonderful view across the river over to Docklands, dominated by Canary Wharf. Down below, the park is elegantly laid out with formal flower gardens and tree-lined avenues. Hidden away is the wilderness area where deer have lived since the fifteenth century.

❖

DLR Island Gardens (then by foot tunnel)
BR Greenwich
❑ 53, 54, 177, 180, 188, 199, 202, 286, 306, 380, 386
〰 from Westminster Pier
P parking areas in Blackheath Avenue and Great Cross Avenue for a total of 326 cars; parking times coincide with traffic gate times
✪ only on main road through park
Open: 7.00 a.m.– 6.00 p.m. or dusk

Richmond Park

Richmond, Surrey TW10

In the reign of Henry VIII, and probably long before, Richmond Park was a hunting area known as Shene Chase. It was Charles I who enclosed it in 1637 as a hunting park he called Richmond New Park – a name that remained in use into the nineteenth century. It was probably given the title 'New' because from Tudor times there had been two other Richmond parks – the 'Great'and

the 'Little'. Not surprisingly, local people bitterly opposed Charles's decision to enclose the park, especially as it meant taking away their common land. As a concession, the king allowed pedestrians the right of way through the park; he placed gates wherever the wall crossed a thoroughfare and put ladders over the walls to preserve access to footpaths. He also stipulated that the poor should be allowed to carry away deadwood from the trees for firewood, as they had done before enclosure.

During the Protectorate, Oliver Cromwell presented the park to the City of London in recognition of the support it had given to his cause during the Civil War, but it was quickly returned to Charles II when he was restored to the throne in 1660. Charles II used it as a hunting area, as his father, Charles I, had before him – both red and fallow deer have always roamed here. Today, two herds of the Queen's deer – 250 red and 350 dappled fallow deer – are allowed to wander free and it is still a treasonous offence to kill a deer, accidentally or otherwise, so drive carefully!

It was William III and his wife, Mary, daughter of James II, who for the first time allowed the public to use the park other than as a right of way, but it was not until 1886 that carriages and later cars were allowed into the park.

The park is known today for its wildlife, its majestic oak trees and the rhododendrons of the Isabella Plantation. From the top of the Henry VII mound (said to have been raised to allow the king to survey the field) there are also marvellous views, extending from Windsor Castle to the dome of St Paul's. Also

Fallow deer in Richmond Park

you do not have to be an athlete to get from one side of the park to the other as there are roads running across and round the perimeter.

Among the houses in the park are Thatched House Lodge, the former home of Princess Alexandra, White Lodge, built by George II in 1727 as a hunting lodge and since 1855 the junior section of the Royal Ballet School, and Pembroke Lodge, a café. This is a lovely place to stop for refreshments; there are pleasant rooms looking out on to the terrace and a dining room (with a fireplace by Robert Adam) in which lunches and afternoon teas are served. Incidentally, the house lies in 5 hectares (13 acres) of its own semi-formal gardens which are worth a wander round. It is open daily during park opening times.

Sports facilities include golf, riding, fishing (permit needed, available from Parks Office on 0171 948 3209) and a flying field for model aeroplanes opposite the polo field on the right-hand side of the road leading to White Lodge.

⊖ Richmond

BR Richmond, Kingston

❑ 57, 65, 72, 74, 85, 170, 213, 265, 371

✪ cycling is allowed on the main roads through the park and on some of the paths

Open: daily 7.00 a.m.–½ hour before dusk

3
LONDON'S WATERWAYS

LONDON'S CANALS

Half hidden in the bustling urban setting of London is the peaceful world of canals. The Grand Union, the Regent's and the Hertford canals swing in a wide arc through the heart of London to link with the River Lee Navigation to the east and the River Thames to the south, with another arm dropping south to Brentford, where it joins the Thames too. Today the whole canal system in London is generally known as the Grand Union Canal. Weaving between factories and warehouses or opening into parks, gardens and nature reserves, it is a fascinating place to explore.

GROWTH, DECLINE AND REVIVAL

The great development of canals started at the time of the Industrial Revolution. The Grand Junction Canal (now known as the Grand Union Main Line) was the first to be built in London, in 1794, and was so called because it linked the Thames with the growing canal network in the Midlands and the North. It ran between Brentford, on the north bank of the Thames opposite Kew, and

Regent's Canal, Little Venice

Braunston in Northamptonshire (150 kilometres/93 miles) to the north. Seven years later a branch of the Grand Junction was opened to Paddington (Paddington Arm), which brought canal traffic almost into the centre of London. By 1820 the canal was extended and barges were now able to reach the dock in east London via Camden and Islington – this part is called Regent's Canal.

However, it was not long before the railways arrived and tempted most of the canal's business away. The invention of motorized transport and the consequent growth of haulage firms dealt the final blow to the canals' commercial existence. As the canals receded in importance, weeds, reeds and rubbish increased at an alarming rate and by the 1950s the central and eastern sections of the canals were virtually derelict. Luckily, the leisure potential of the canals was finally realized. The British Waterways Board was formed in 1963 to manage the country's entire canal network and helped to focus attention on restoration, preservation and conservation, as well as developing recreational use. The canals that have survived today are all part of the Grand Union Canal system and the River Lee Navigation canals.

EXPLORING THE CANALS

There are plenty of ways to enjoy the canals: leave the crowded streets and take a quiet stroll along the towpath or simply enjoy a relaxing boat trip. Apart from short stretches, such as the tunnels at Islington and Maida Hill and the Limehouse Cut, it is possible to walk along most of London's 87 kilometres (54 miles) of towpaths (see page 77). There are many access points, all close to bus routes or underground stations, so you can go for either a short walk or a long-distance ramble. A booklet giving detailed information on canal walks is available from the Regent's Canal Information Centre, which will also provide details of guided walks.

If you are feeling lazy, there are regular boat trips through Regent's Park, between Little Venice and Camden, or along the Regent's Canal to the junction with the River Thames at Limehouse. For the more energetic, there are plenty of facilities for watersports (see also page 142). Listed below are some interesting sights along the central part of London's canals, from Little Venice to Limehouse Basin.

Little Venice

W2

Little Venice, where the Regent's Canal joins the Paddington Arm of the Grand Union Canal to form a large pool, is a good starting point for exploring London's canals, either by boat or on foot. Around the pool are some splendid Georgian houses, which look down on colourful narrow boats and barges moored along the banks. Browning's Island, named after the poet Robert Browning, stands in the centre, forming a haven for ducks, geese and swans beneath its weeping willows.

θ Warwick Avenue

❏ 6, 18, 46

Lazy days, by Tube
at Little Venice. Nearest station: Warwick Avenue

Maida Hill Tunnel

Maida Vale, W9

This is a 'legging' tunnel through which there is no towpath. Spoil from the tunnel excavation was laid on the field of a nearby landowner, Thomas Lord. The field was later to become the world-famous Lord's Cricket Ground.

Regent's Park

Off Prince Albert Road, Albany Street, Marylebone Road and Park Road, Marylebone, NW1

The Regent's Canal sweeps through the northern section of Regent's Park and London Zoo in a deep, tree-lined cutting, providing one of the most spectacular views on London's canals. On one side is the famous Snowdon Aviary and the antelope terraces can be seen on the other.

Macclesfield Bridge

Regent's Park, NW1

Now known as 'Blow-up Bridge', this was the scene of an explosion in 1874 when a barge carrying a cargo of gunpowder ignited as it was passing underneath. The original bridge columns were used to rebuild the bridge but they were re-erected the wrong way round, so the marks worn by the towing ropes are today on the wrong side.

Cumberland Basin

Regent's Park, NW1

Today this is a mooring area and the site of a restaurant. Originally the basin formed the junction of the Regent's Canal main line, with a 1.2-kilometre (¾-mile) arm that led off round the park to Cumberland Hay Market, near Euston Road. This branch was filled in with war rubble in 1948 and the London Zoo car park is now on top of it. To the right is St Mark's church, Regent's Park.

Camden Lock

Camden, NW1

Once a timber wharf and dock, this area has now been converted into a thriving craft and canal centre with shops, restaurants, boat trips, a cruising restaurant boat and a bustling weekend market.

Camden Lock

St Pancras Lock

King's Cross, N1

In dramatic contrast to its urban surroundings, the canal creates a picturesque waterside setting as it passes behind the busy King's Cross and St Pancras railway stations. Just south of St Pancras Basin, next to the canal, is the Camley Street Natural Park, a nature area managed by the London Wildlife Trust. The park houses a wildlife habitat of ponds, marsh, meadow, scrub and woodland. You can also follow the 'newt trail' from the canal towpath to reach the park entrance (see also page 90).

London Canal Museum

12/13 New Wharf Road, King's Cross, N1 (0171 713 0836)

Although this is not strictly outdoors, it is an interesting place to visit during a walk along the canal. The museum tells the history of the development of London's canals and gives a fascinating insight into the people who strove to make a living from their boats.

It is housed in a former warehouse built in the 1850s for Carlo Gatti, a famous ice-cream manufacturer. Blocks of ice were imported from Norway and carried on the Regent's Canal from the dock at Limehouse to Battlebridge Basin. Beneath the warehouse there are two vast ice wells, one of which has been partly excavated and is now on show to the public.

⊖ Kings Cross

❑ 10, C12, 17, 18, 30, 45, 46, 63, 73, 91, 214, 221, 259

Open: Tuesday–Sunday, 10.00 a.m.– 4.30 p.m., all bank holidays except 24–26 December, 1 and 2 January

£

City Road Basin

Off City Road, Islington, EC1

Opened in 1820, City Road was the principal basin on this stretch of canal, serving many wharves and factories. Today it is a popular watersports centre.

Victoria Park

Old Ford Road and Grove Road, South Hackney, E9

This famous East End park, London's oldest municipal park, leads right down to the edge of Regent's Canal. The park covers 88 hectares (217 acres) (see also page 39).

Limehouse Basin

Limehouse, E14

Limehouse Basin was once a busy terminus where goods were transferred from ships to canal boats. With declining commercial use, the basin became redundant. Today it is a wildlife oasis and for the first time for over 100 years you will be able to see birds such as the great crested glebe and tufted duck here.

BR/DLR Limehouse

❑ 5, D9, P14, 15, 15B, 40

GRAND UNION AND REGENT'S CANALS' CRUISES

Colne Valley Passenger Boat Service

Denham Marina, 100 Acres, Sanderson Road, Uxbridge, Middlesex UB8 1NB (01895 812130)

The *Farnworth*, a converted coal boat from the Leeds and Liverpool Canal, now

provides a variety of private charter and public trips between April and October. Trips take place on Sunday and Wednesday afternoons and there are also special Christmas trips in December.
££

The Floating Boater

1 Bishops Bridge Road, London W2 6ND (0171 724 8740)
Two charter boats – *Lapwing* and *Prince Regent* – run from Little Venice to Regent's Park, catering for groups and parties. Both can be hired out at lunchtime or evening for up to four hours. *Prince Regent* holds just under 100 people and offers a more extensive, hot menu. *Lapwing* holds up to fifty people and offers buffet/cold food only.
Trip times: Lapwing, March–September; *Prince Regent,* March–December
££

Jason's Trip

60 Blomfield Road, Little Venice, London W9 2PA (0171 286 3428)
Since 1951, Jason's Trip has been taking visitors along the canal from Little Venice to Camden Lock market on traditional narrow boats. At their base in Little Venice, you can wait for your boat in a delightful courtyard where there is a small coffee shop. In the summer there are also inclusive teatime cruises with afternoon tea, and evening cruises with traditional fish and chips. Trips are available to the London Canal Museum as well.
Trip times: April–May, 10.30 a.m., 12.30 p.m., 2.30 p.m.; June–August, 10.30 a.m., 12.30 p.m., 2.30 p.m., 4.30 p.m. (weekends and bank holidays only); September, 10.30 a.m., 12.30 p.m., 2.30 p.m.; October: 12.30 p.m., 2.30 p.m.
££

Jenny Wren and My Fair Lady

250 Camden High Street, London NW1 8QS (0171 485 4433)
Jenny Wren makes a round trip from Camden Town past London Zoo and Regent's Park, to Little Venice and back, with an interesting commentary on the canal's history.
Trip times: March–October (weekends and school holidays), 11.30 a.m., 2.00 p.m., 3.30 p.m.; November–February (weekends, weather permitting), times vary so phone
££
My Fair Lady was built as a cruising restaurant in the manner of the traditional Broads canal boats. The trips run to Little Venice and back and include a three-course meal *en route.*
Trip times: dinner cruise Tuesday–Saturday, 7.30 p.m.;
lunch cruise Sundays only, 12.30 p.m.
££

Lady Rose of Regent's

Canal Office, Little Venice, London W2 6ND (0171 286 3428)
Traditional narrow boats run from Little Venice to Camden Lock from the beginning of April to the end of October. Food is available on board if you preorder and there is a bar too.

Trip times: April–September weekdays, 12.30 p.m., 2.30 p.m. and weekends, 10.30 a.m., 12.30 p.m., 2.30 p.m.; June–August weekdays, 12.30 p.m., 2.30 p.m., 4.30 p.m. and weekends, 10.30 a.m., 12.30 p.m., 2.30 p.m., 4.30 p.m.; October, weekends only, 10.30 a.m., 12.30 p.m., 2.30 p.m.
££

London Waterbus Company

Camden Lock, London NW1 8AF (0171 482 2550)
Using three traditional painted narrow boats, there is a scheduled service between Little Venice and Camden Lock. There are also special day trips across north and east London, including King's Cross, Islington and Victoria Park and then on either to the River Lea or to Limehouse Basin.
Trip times: boats depart every hour in summer and every 1½ hours in winter (weekends only)

RIVER LEA AND STORT BOAT CRUISES

Lee Valley Regional Park Authority

Myddleton House, Bulls Cross, Enfield, Middlesex EN2 9HG (01992 717711)
You can explore the rivers Lea and Stort on any of five cruising boats listed below. They are heated and equipped with bar, catering facilities and toilets.

Adventuress Cruises, Unit X, The Maltings, Station Road, Sawbridgeworth, Hertfordshire CM21 9LB (01279 600848)
Adventuress plies the River Stort and is equipped to provide a wide range of cruises.
££

Hazlemere Marine, Highbridge Street, Waltham Abbey, Essex EN10 7AX (01992 768013)
The *Hazlemere* is a cruising restaurant boat, with regular scheduled Sunday lunches and Friday and Saturday dinner cruises.
££

Lee and Stort Waterbus Navigation Co. Ltd, The Bollards, 30 Goldsworthy Drive, Great Wakering, Essex SS3 0AU (01920 487999)
The traditionally painted narrow boat *Wind in the Willows* operates a weekend water-bus service on the Stort. A live commentary is provided and bar and light refreshments are available.
££

Lee Valley Marina, Springfield Marina, Spring Hill, Clapton, E5 9BL (0181 806 1717)
Pride of Lee offers the ideal way to discover the lower reaches of the Lea and London's water-way heritage. There are plenty of places to visit and pubs to stop at en route.
££

Lee Valley Narrowboat Co. Ltd, The Lock Keeper's Cottage, Amwell Lane, Stanstead Abbotts, Nr Ware, Hertfordshire SG12 8DR (01920 870068)

Jonas Fosbrooke was originally built for a television company to entertain their VIPS. Today, it is available to the public for cruises along the Rivers Lea and Stort. **££**

BOATING AND CANOEING

If you want to take your own boat, powered or unpowered, on the canal, you will need a British Waterways' licence. However, there is also a Community Boats scheme – ideal for schools and youth groups – whereby it is possible to hire boats for a half-day, a day or even a weekend break. Listed below are organizations which hire out boats on the canals and on the rivers Lea and Stort.

RIVERS LEA AND STORT

Rowing boats and motor boats are available for hourly hire. Cabin cruisers are available for hourly, day or weekend hire.
££

Planck Burrett Marina
Station Road, Bishop's Stortford, Hertfordshire (01279 434080)
Paddle boats, rowing boats and motors boats are available for hourly hire. Fully enclosed electric boats seating eight are available for half-day and full-day hire.
££

Lee Valley Boat Centre
Old Nazeing Road, Broxbourne, Hertfordshire (01992 462085)
A variety of boats is available for hire, including self-drive narrow boats, which are available for weekly and three-day hire.
££

RIVER THAMES

Travelling up the Thames from Greenwich to Hampton Court is one of the most pleasurable ways of seeing London, and one of the most relaxing. Upstream, after the splendours of Westminster, the City and the Tower of London, the scene changes to the warehouses and docks of the Pool of London, ending in the open spaces of Greenwich and the Royal Naval College. Going inland, the most attractive downstream stretch of the river begins in Putney, past the urban landscape of Chelsea. You can also walk from here, along a mostly riverside walk, all the way to Kew, starting on the south bank at Putney and crossing over to the north at Hammersmith. All along the length of the River Thames are small islands. These are known as aits or ayots, such as Richmond Ait and Ravens Ait. Many are uninhabited and have become small island wildlife reserves.

All along the Thames you pass aspects of every part of London life, from parks, pubs, warehouses and bridges to famous landmarks, such as Hampton Court, Greenwich, Lambeth Palace and the Tower of London. Plenty of guided tours are available to find out more about them, and below are just a few of the most important sights to look out for or to stop and explore along the river. This section deals with river trips. For more details on river walks, see pages 74–5 and for sports facilities, such as sailing, canoeing and rowing, see pages 142–5.

UPSTREAM FROM WESTMINSTER PIER TO DOCKLANDS

Westminster Pier and Bridge

SW1 (North)
The inspiration for Wordsworth's sonnet in 1807, the current Westminster Bridge is the successor to the stone original of 1750, which was the next bridge to be built after London Bridge.

The Houses of Parliament

St Margaret Street, SW1 (North)
The Palace of Westminster (generally known as the Houses of Parliament) was rebuilt from 1834 onwards, after a fire destroyed most of the original buildings. The only parts to have survived are the Great Hall, built by William II between 1097 and 1099, and the crypt and cloisters of St Stephen's Chapel.

The palace was a royal residence from the reign of Edward the Confessor to the reign of Henry VII and it is now the seat of government. The buildings are vast, covering 3 hectares (8 acres), with eleven courtyards, 3 kilometres (2 miles) of passages and over 1,000 rooms. Big Ben, the most famous clock tower in Britain, was probably named after Sir Benjamin Hall, who commissioned the enormous bell and completed work on the 97-metre (316-foot) tower in 1859.

Cleopatra's Needle

Victoria Embankment, WC2 (North)
Originally erected in Egypt around 1500 BC, this monument was presented to Britain in 1819 in recognition of her help during the Battle of the Nile in 1798. However, it was some sixty years before it arrived in London. It stands 21 metres (68 feet) high.

The South Bank Centre

Upper Ground, SE1 (South)
The South Bank Centre has become one of the most controversial examples of post-war architecture since it was first developed for the Festival of Britain in 1951.

Love it or hate it, it is one of the most important centres for the arts in London and includes the Royal Festival Hall, the Royal National Theatre, the National Film Theatre, the Purcell Room, the Hayward Gallery and the Queen Elizabeth Hall.

Waterloo Bridge
WC2
This bridge was designed in 1945 by G. G. Scott, replacing John Rennie's nineteenth century version.

Somerset House
Strand, WC2 (North)
These elegant buildings are home to the Courtauld Institute galleries. Somerset House dates from 1776. Queen Elizabeth I lived in the palace that formerly stood here.

St Paul's Cathedral
Ludgate Hill, EC4 (North)
One of London's most imposing skylines shows the dignified dome of St Paul's Cathedral surrounded by the futuristic skyscrapers and buildings of the City, all the more impressive when seen from the river. St Paul's was designed by Sir Christopher Wren, after the original was destroyed by the Great Fire of London in 1666, and it took forty-two years to complete.

St Paul's Cathedral

London Bridge
EC4
London Bridge was the only crossing over the lower Thames until 1750, when Westminster Bridge was finished. Originally constructed by the Romans, it has been rebuilt several times and the present one dates from 1973. Its predecessor, built by the engineer John Rennie in 1831, was sold for £1m and is now situated in Arizona in the USA. The story goes that the owner thought London Bridge was Tower Bridge and, therefore, bought the wrong one, although he claims he had always intended to buy London Bridge!

Overleaf: The Thames

HMS Belfast

Hay's Galleria, Vine Lane, Tooley Street, SE1 (South) (0171 407 6434)
The *Belfast* (11,500 tons) was a World War II cruiser that saw service with the Arctic convoys and on D-day. Today, visitors can enjoy exploring the ship. Other ships to be seen in this stretch of the river include a World War II frigate, *Wellington*, the floating Livery Hall of the Honourable Company of Master Mariner, two First World War sloops, *Chrysanthemum* and *President*, headquarters of the London division of the RNVR and RNR.

⊖/**BR** London Bridge
❏ DI, P3, DII, PII, 17, 21, 22A, 35, 40, 43, X43, 47, 48, 133, 344, 501, 521
Open: daily, 11.00 a.m.–5.50 p.m. (4.30 p.m. in winter)
£

HMS Belfast

Tower of London

Tower Hill, EC3 (North) (0171 709 0765)
One of the most famous landmarks in London, the Tower has been a palace, a prison, a mint and now holds the Crown Jewels. It was built by William I in 1078 on a vantage point on the river to defend the city from invaders.

Guided tours are given by yeoman warders (popularly known as Beefeaters). The nightly Ceremony of the Keys can be watched only by written application to the Governor's Office, Queen's House, HM Tower of London, EC3N 4AB (see also page 184).

⊖ Tower Hill
DLR Tower Hill (Monday–Friday, 5.30 a.m.–12.00 a.m.)
❏ DI, D9, DII, 15, 25, 42, 78, 100
Open: March–October, Monday–Saturday, 9.30 a.m.–5.30 p.m., Sunday, 2.00 p.m.–5.00p.m.; November–February, Monday–Saturday, 9.30 a.m. –4.00 p.m., closed Sundays in winter
££

Tower Bridge from St Katharine's Dock

Tower Bridge
SE1 (0171 403 3761)
There are splendid views from the enclosed high-level walkway across the top of the towers – you can either walk up the 200 steps or take the lift. There is also a museum with various interesting exhibits, plus Victorian engine rooms with the original steam engines, which used to open the bridge to let ships through. Today, the hydraulic lifting mechanisms are powered by electricity.
⊖ London Bridge, Tower Hill
DLR Tower Hill (Monday–Friday, 5.30 a.m.–12.00 a.m.)
❏ D1, P3, D9, D11, P11, 15, 17, 21, 22A, 25, 35, 40, 42, 43, X43, 47, 48, 78, 100, 133, 344, 501, 521
Open: April–October daily, 10.00 a.m.–6.30 p.m.; November–March, 10.00 a.m.–4.45 p.m.
££

St Katharine's Dock
E1 (North)
Opened in 1826 by Thomas Telford to handle valuable cargoes, such as ivory and silver, it was redeveloped in the 1980s to include the World Trade Centre, a large hotel and an exclusive yacht marina. Also home to the Dickens Inn, one of the oldest pubs in London (see also page 169) and to RRS *Discovery,* Captain Scott's vessel.

The Isle of Dogs
E14 (North)
Canary Wharf now dominates this part of the regenerated Docklands, bringing a new lease of life to what was an industrial wasteland.

❖

Greenwich (South)

The river gives the best view of Wren's superb Royal Naval College (originally a naval hospital). Besides the college sits the *Cutty Sark* in dry dock. The famous clipper carried wool, tea, redwood and sugar from Australia and could sail over 1,600 kilometres (1,000 miles) in three days.

Gypsy Moth IV

This tiny 11-metre (35-foot) yacht was sailed single-handed around the world by Sir Francis Chichester – the first ever solo circumnavigation.

THE DOCKLANDS

Stretching along both banks of the Thames to the east of the City of London, are London's docklands – the site of the largest urban regeneration project in Europe. This was once the heart of London's thriving world port, and the riverside was originally lined with wharves and warehouses. Huge docks were built on both sides of the river, hidden away behind high walls.

For many years the docks were in a state of disuse and decline, but now a programme of regeneration has meant there is a strikingly new view of the main docklands on the north bank of the Thames and developments such as the giant Canary Wharf rub shoulders with historic pubs and refurbished warehouses. Once away from the river, you can explore the docklands on the north side by Docklands Light Railway (DLR) or on a guided tour from the London Docklands Development Corporation (LDDC) Visitor Centre, 3 Lime Harbour, E14 on the Isle of Dogs (0171 512 3000).

EXPLORING THE DOCKLANDS

One of the surprises of docklands is the number of parks and walks, many of them along the river or around conserved docks. The Victorian riverside parks at North Woolwich and Island Gardens in Shadwell have retained their formal flowerbeds beneath canopies of mature trees.

In contrast, the more recent parks like John McDougall Park on the Isle of Dogs and Pearsons Park in Surrey Docks are the work of modern landscape architects, with more exotic species in a contoured setting leading up to the riverside walks and views. The LDDC hopes to link all these parks into a continuous walk. The Countryside Commission recently decided to include Dockland's emerging riverside route in its designated long-distance footpath, the Thames Path (see also page 80).

There are many walks around the historic areas of Docklands. The LDDC has produced heritage trails both for the Isle of Dogs and Surrey Docks and these are available at the Visitor Centre.

The Surrey Docks pedestrian trail is now signposted, with displays which explain the history of the immediate locality. It is a 2½-hour walk or a shorter cycle ride. Apart from the historic interest, the walk is enhanced by the green spaces of Surrey Docks, particularly Russia Dock Woodland and the emerging ecological park.

❖

Docklands Tours
60 Bradley House, Aspinden Road,
Bermondsey, SE16 (0171 252 0742)
Guided coach, minibus and walking tours
of the dockland area, by local people.
££

The Pirate Ships
1–2 Tobacco Dock, E1 (0171 702 9681)
This is a fun museum/exhibition depicting
the story of piracy and life at sea.
⊖ Wapping
⊖/**DLR** Shadwell (Monday–Friday, 5.30a.m.–12.00 a.m.)
❑ DI, D9, DI I, 100
Open: daily, 10.00 a.m.–5.30 p.m.
££

Thames Barrier Visitors' Centre
Unity Way, Woolwich, SE18 (South) (0181 854 1375)
The Thames Barrier is a magnificent construction built in 1984 to protect
London from major floods. The capital certainly needs these important defences:
in 1928 fourteen people drowned in central London and in 1953 there was a
disastrous flood along the east coast and Thames estuary, with the loss of 300 lives.
If the flood had reached central London, the results could have been even more
disastrous. An informative exhibition and spectacular audio–visual show explain
the history, construction and operation of London's tidal flood defences.
⊖ New Cross, New Cross Gate
BR Charlton or Greenwich, then shuttle service
❑ 177, 180
〰 regular services from Westminster Pier (75 minutes) and Greenwich (25
minutes); a Round-Barrier Boat Cruise (tel: 0181 854 5555) runs from Barrier
Gardens Pier, with full commentary on the Barrier and local geography (30
minutes)
Open: 1 April–30 September, daily, 10.30 a.m.–5.00 p.m.; 1 October–31 March, daily,
10.30 a.m.–5.00 p.m.

DOWNSTREAM FROM WESTMINSTER BRIDGE
TO HAMPTON COURT

Battersea Park
See page 27

Royal Hospital, Chelsea
SW3 (North)
The Royal Hospital in Chelsea was founded by Charles II in the 1680s as a retreat
for veterans of the regular army who had become unfit for duty, either after twenty

years' service or as a result of serious injuries. It is still run on the same military lines today and is home for about 400 Chelsea Pensioners, who wear their traditional red uniform.

Hurlingham Club

Ranelagh Gardens, SW6 (North)
The stretch of gardens and grounds on the right just before Putney Bridge belongs to the Hurlingham Club, once a famous polo ground and now an exclusive club with a long waiting list (up to six years).

Putney Bridge

SW6
This is the starting point of the annual Oxford and Cambridge Boat Race (see page 188) and the centre of activity for a multitude of rowing clubs which have their boathouses here. Beside the river are the elegant grounds of Fulham Palace. Originally the Bishops of London's private grounds, they are now a public park (see also pages 42 and 110).

Hammersmith and Chiswick (North)

Between Hammersmith and Chiswick are a succession of attractive, riverside roads and paths, known as 'malls', where some of the most attractive buildings in London can be found. Just by Hammersmith Bridge is the Dove, a popular riverside pub (see page 181), followed by a row of Georgian houses, many with distinguished associations. Particularly notable are Morton House, Strawberry House and Walpole House – thought possibly to be 'Miss Pinkerton's Academy' in the novel *Vanity Fair*. William Morris started his printing press at Kelmscott House on Hammersmith Mall in 1891, naming it after his Oxfordshire home. Chiswick Mall ends at Chiswick Ferry landing, with St Nicholas Church just back from the river, where Hogarth is buried.

Strand-on-the-Green

W4 (North)
Just before Kew Bridge is Strand-on-the-Green – a slight misnomer as the only green is a strip of grass between the road and the footway. The area has an attractive,

Hammersmith Bridge
W6
The first bridge here was built by Tierney Clark in 1827 and was the earliest suspension bridge across the Thames. This was replaced by a new bridge in the 1840s, which was developed by Sir Joseph Bazalgette, who was also responsible for the Thames embankments.

There is a wooden handrail on the upstream side of the bridge in honour of Charles Wood, an officer in the Royal Air Force who saved a woman from drowning by diving off this bridge.

❖

village-like atmosphere and the row of houses looking on to the river is almost unchanged since it was built in the eighteenth century. Many were built in the same period as Chiswick Mall, although some were originally fishermen's cottages rather than grand homes. The most important house here belonged to the artist Johann Zoffany.

Syon House and Park
Brentford, Middlesex (North)
Facing Kew Gardens from across the river is Syon House and Park. The house was built on the site of a Brigittine convent soon after Henry VIII's Dissolution of the Monasteries and it has belonged to the Dukes and Earls of Northumberland since the Reformation – the Northumberland lion can be clearly seen on the roofline. Inside is a splendid interior designed by Robert Adam, while outside the gardens are worth are a separate visit (see page 115). Beyond Syon Park is Isleworth village, with its famous pub, the London Apprentice, on the river bank.

The City Barge, Strand-on-the-Green

Kew Gardens
Kew, Surrey TW9 (South)
See Royal Botanic Gardens page 113

Richmond Waterfront
Richmond, Surrey TW10 (South)
Richmond's waterfront was designed by Quinlan Terry in the 1980s and provides an imposing view from the river of this historic town. Riddled with royal associations, Richmond boasts a wealth of Georgian architecture, an elegant green, smart shops and an impressive view of the curving Thames from the top of Richmond Hill. For more information on Richmond Park see page 53.

Ham House and Marble Hill House
Ham, Surrey TW10 (South) and Twickenham, Middlesex TW1 (North)
Ham House is a beautiful Stuart house, built about 1610, which stands back from the river on the left bank just before Eel Pie Island and Teddington Lock, on one of the most unspoiled stretches of river bank before Hampton Court. It was built by Sir Thomas Vavasour in 1610, with many additions made throughout the seventeenth century by the Earl of Dysart and later by the Duke of Lauderdale.

❖

The gardens have recently been redesigned by the National Trust and planted to the original seventeenth-century plan (see page 117).

If you visit the house and gardens by road, you can take a small ferry and hop over to the Twickenham side and visit the park and grounds of Marble Hill House, a Palladian house built for George II's mistress, the Countess of Suffolk, in about 1725 and later occupied by Mrs Fitzherbert, the mistress of George IV. The building has now been restored and concerts are held in the grounds on Sunday evenings in July and August (see also page 155).

Teddington Lock
Teddington, Middlesex TW11
The weir here is the longest on the Thames, and is important as from this spot the river is non-tidal and keeps a fairly constant level.

Hampton Court Palace and Gardens

See page 51

RIVER TRIPS AND SIGHTSEEING TOURS

Numerous cruise boats take tours up and down the river and are reasonably priced. For recorded information on river trips phone 0839 123432 or contact the piers direct on the phone numbers given below:

Charing Cross Pier, Victoria Embankment, WC2 (0171 839 3572)
To Greenwich and Tower of London, also evening cruises.
⊖ Embankment
❑ 6, 9, 11, 13, 15, 23, 91, 176
££

Tower Pier, Tower Hill, EC3 (0171 488 0344)
To Westminster and Greenwich, with a ferry to HMS *Belfast*.
⊖ Tower Hill
❑ D1, D9, D11, 15, 25, 42, 78, 100
££

Westminster Pier, Victoria Embankment, SW1
Downstream to Greenwich (0171 930 4097) and Tower Bridge (0171 930 9033).
Upstream to Hampton Court, Kew, Putney and Richmond (0171 930 2062/4721). Also circular cruises and evening and lunch cruises.
⊖ Westminster
❑ 3, 11, 12, 24, 53, 77A, 88, 109, 159, 211
££

Opposite: Richmond waterfront

4
URBAN AND GREEN WALKS

L ONDON does not at first seem to lend itself to casual strolls, at least in the centre, but there are some excellent self-guided walks you can follow, such as the Silver Jubilee Walk, which take you past all sorts of interesting sights and keep you away from the crowds. There are also a number of companies which run themed walking tours; these are great fun, even in the rain, as the guides are always entertaining and the walkers tend to be very sociable.

Many of the excellent self-guided walks are the result of much hard work by the London Walking Forum, which opens up new green walks in and around London. The Forum is a partnership between the Countryside Commission, the Sports Council, local authorities and recreational interests across London and began its work in 1990. Its aim is to link together all the green spaces, the paths along river banks and other green routes in London so that people can go for country-style strolls without having to negotiate congested urban streets. This dream has led pioneering local authorities to develop the first country-style walks in London, such as the Green Chain Walk and the Regent's Canal Walk (see below and page 77).

Setting standards is a very important part of the Forum's work. Routes carry the 'London Walks' logo as well as their own waymarking. In addition, routes will soon all have guide leaflets to tell you where to go, which sections are suitable for wheelchairs and buggies, what the main attractions are and so on. The London Walks Forum is still in its early stages and Londoners can help ensure its success by trying out the first approved walks and then encouraging local authorities to improve or create new routes near their homes.

Also, many country parks and some of the larger London parks mentioned earlier run their own circular walks, which are listed. Contact the individual parks for more information and leaflets.

SELF-GUIDED WALKS

Green Chain Walk
The Green Chain comprises a string of nearly 300 of the finest open spaces in south-east London, including parks, gardens, woods, commons, playing fields, golf courses and farmland. Its aim is to preserve and enhance these open spaces, prevent further building from taking place and improve sport and recreation facilities here. The Green Chain Walk is a 63-kilometre (39-mile) waymarked walk linking them all from Thamesmead to Beckenham, through the boroughs of Bexley, Greenwich, Lewisham and Bromley.

The walks are broken up into manageable chunks of about 6.5 kilometres (4 miles) each, so you can start where you like. You will pass some wonderful views, as well as numerous historic sites, such as Eltham Palace, built in 1475, which has an impressive Great Hall and moat bridge, and the ruined monastery in Lesnes Abbey Woods. Other noteworthy sites include Charlton Park and House, one of the best examples of Jacobean architecture in the country, and Severndroog Castle – a magnificent folly erected in 1784.

Four leaflets cover the whole of the route.

I. Thamesmead to Oxleas Wood (or Erith)
This walk covers just under 10 kilometres (6 miles) from the riverside promenade on the south bank of the Thames at Thamesmead, through Lesnes Woods to Oxleas Wood and Shooters Hill, along part of the old Roman Road to London (see also page 37). A 4-kilometre (2½-mile) branch from the riverside at Erith connecting with the main route at Lesnes Abbey is also described.

2. Thames Barrier to Oxleas Woods (or Bostall Woods)
This is a 7-kilometre (4¼-mile) walk from the Thames Barrier on the south side of the River Thames, via Charlton Park to Oxleas Wood and Shooters Hill. Another walk of just under 6.5 kilometres (4 miles) from Charlton Park via Plumstead Common to Bostall Woods, connecting with the Thamesmead route, is also described. This link encompasses a 10-kilometre (6-mile) circular walk.

3. Oxleas Wood to Mottingham
It is 6.5 kilometres (4 miles) from start to finish on this walk, although there are alternative longer and shorter routes: a western route through Eltham Park South and an eastern route almost 1.6 kilometres (1 mile) longer through Avery Hill Park and New Eltham. A short link between the two routes connecting Conduit Head with Avery Hill Park allows for two circular walks of 5 and 6 kilometres (3 and 3¾ miles) to be made.

4. Mottingham to Crystal Palace Park (or Chislehurst)
This is a much longer walk, covering 13 kilometres (8 miles). Alternative routes are provided between Mottingham and Beckenham Place Park, with a northern walk through Grove Park and Downham and a southern section, 1 kilometre (½ mile) longer between Elmstead Woods and Sundridge Park. A link between the two routes connecting Grove Park Hospital through Chinbrook Meadows to Elmstead Woods allows for two circular walks of 5 and 10.5 kilometres (3 and 6½ miles) to be made. A 3-kilometre (1¾-mile) branch from Elmstead Woods to Chislehurst Common is also described.

Leaflets and more detailed information on all these walks are available from the Director of Leisure Services, Bromley Civic Centre, Rochester Avenue, Bromley, Kent BR1 3UH (tel: 0181 464 3333). In addition to the walks information, a general leaflet containing a fold-out map of the Green Chain, with a summary of planning policies, is also available from the same address.

BR Abbey Wood, Beckenham Hill, Belvedere, Crystal Palace, Eltham, Falconwood, Grove Park, Mottingham, New Eltham, Welling, Woolwich Dockyard

❖

Brent River Walk

Ealing, Hanwell and Brentford
See also page 89
There are five interesting circular walks along Brent River Park, a chain of green spaces along the River Brent in west London. These take you through woodland and open space as well as past the unusual 'canal staircase' flight of locks at Hanwell.

For more information, contact the Park Ranger on 0181 566 1929 or visit the Brent River Environmental Centre, Brent Lodge Park, Church Road, W7.
BR Drayton Green, Hanwell, South Greenford

Bromley Walks

As well as participating in the Green Chain Walks, Bromley Council has created a fascinating series of self-guided circular walks throughout the borough and produced a set of useful leaflets to accompany them. As one of London's largest and most 'rural' boroughs there is plenty of countryside to explore and the leaflets, packed with useful information and maps, are essential guides.

1. Cudham Circular Walk

A 5.5-kilometre (3½-mile) walk from Cudham to the High Elms Estates and back.
BR Orpington
❑ R1, R2, R3, R4, R5, R6, R7, R8, R11, 51, 61, 208, 353, 493,

2. Nash Circular Walk

A 7-kilometre (4½-mile) walk through attractive, rolling countryside, passing through the old commons of Hayes and Keston.
BR Bromley North
❑ 61, 119, 126, 138, 146, 162, 208, 227, 261, 269, 314, 320, 336, 354, 367, 402, 726

3. Chelsfield Circular Walk

A 9-kilometre (5½-mile) walk starting at Chelsfield Green and passing through Goddington Park, woodland and farmland.
BR Chelsfield
❑ R3, 493

4. Leaves Green Circular Walk

This 10.5-kilometre (6½-mile) walk passes through the villages of Leaves Green and Downe and into the attractive surrounding countryside. There is also a shorter walk around Leaves Green Common and the village which takes about 30–40 minutes and would be suitable for the less energetic.
BR Bromley North
❑ 61, 119, 126, 138, 146, 162, 208, 227, 261, 269, 314, 320, 336, 354, 367, 402, 726

5. Farnborough Circular Walk

Two circular walks, one 7 kilometres (4½ miles) and the other 1.6 kilometres (1 mile) long, take you through Farnborough and out into the countryside beyond.
BR Bromley North
❑ 61, 119, 126, 138, 146, 162, 208, 227, 261, 269, 314, 320, 336, 354, 367, 402, 726

For more information on all these walks and for leaflets, contact the Bromley Civic Centre (see page 75 for the address).

Canal Walk

It is now possible to walk 64 kilometres (40 miles) along the towpaths of the Grand Union Canal and Regent's Canal from Limehouse in the docklands to Rickmansworth. Some 10 kilometres (6 miles) are along the Brentford arm of the Grand Union, while the remainder forms a part of Mile End Park, Victoria Park (page 39), Regent's Park (page 49) and Primrose Hill (page 25), Horsenden Hill (page 93) and 11 kilometres (7 miles) of the Colne Valley Park (see below). A booklet covering canal walks is available from the London Canals Project Officer, British Waterways, Canal Office, Delamare Terrace, London W2 6ND (tel: 0171 289 9897). See also pages 55–60.

Regent's Canal

Colne Valley Circular Walks

The Colne Valley on the western tip of London offers a real taste of the countryside only a few miles from the city. The Colne Valley Park Groundwork Trust has organized eight circular walks through the valley, which are listed below. Varying in length from 5 to 10 kilometres (3 to 6 miles), they explore some of the area's most interesting countryside, including wildlife areas, waterways and historic sites.

1. Nine Stiles

An 8-kilometre (5-mile) walk, taking between 2 and 2½ hours, through farmland and alongside the Grand Union Canal near Uxbridge and Denham.

2. Iver

A 9-kilometre (5½-mile) waterside walk taking about 3 hours, following parts of the Colne and Fray's rivers, the Grand Union Canal and Little Britain Lake.

3. Wraysbury

A 7-kilometre (4½-mile) river and lakeside walk, taking about 2 hours, following parts of the River Thames, Colne Brook and Wraysbury lakes.

4. Harefield Heights

A 10- or 5-kilometre (6- or 3-mile) walk, taking 3 to 3½ hours, through the chalk farmland and alongside the Grand Union Canal near Rickmansworth and Harefield (shorter route 1½ hours).

5. Staines Moor

A 6-kilometre (3½-mile) walk, taking 1½ to 2 hours, across the open grassland of Staines Moor, following part of the Thames, Wraysbury and Colne rivers.

6. Old Shire Lane

A 13- or 7-kilometre (8- or 4½-mile) walk, taking 4 to 4½ hours, through the chalk farmland and woods in the Chilterns, partly following the route of the Old Shire Lane (shorter route 2 to 2½ hours).

7. Chalfont Park

A 10-kilometre (6-mile) walk, taking 3 hours, through open countryside in the Chilterns.

8. Widewater Lock

A 10-kilometre (6-mile) walk, taking 3 hours, along part of the Grand Union Canal, across open countryside and through ancient woodland.

For useful brochures about all these walks and information about becoming a member of the Trust, contact Colne Valley Park Groundwork Trust, Colne Valley Park Centre, Denham Country Park, Denham, Middlesex UB9 5NW (tel: 01895 832662).

Epping Forest Centenary Walk

This 24-kilometre (15-mile) walk along the length of this beautiful forest was devised in 1978 to celebrate the centenary of the saving of the forest from extinction by the City of London. Starting at Manor Park Station, the walk crosses 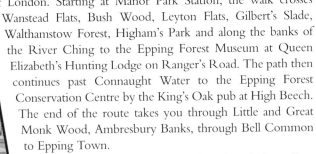 Wanstead Flats, Bush Wood, Leyton Flats, Gilbert's Slade, Walthamstow Forest, Higham's Park and along the banks of the River Ching to the Epping Forest Museum at Queen Elizabeth's Hunting Lodge on Ranger's Road. The path then continues past Connaught Water to the Epping Forest Conservation Centre by the King's Oak pub at High Beech. The end of the route takes you through Little and Great Monk Wood, Ambresbury Banks, through Bell Common to Epping Town.

If the thought of trying to complete the whole walk at one go sounds a little daunting, do not panic! There are good transport facilities along the way for anyone wanting to skip sections. A detailed leaflet about the walk is available from the Information Officer, Epping Forest Conservation Centre, High Beech Road, Loughton, Essex IG10 4BL (tel: 0181 508 7714). See also page 35.

Epping Forest

Lee Valley Park Walks

See also page 37

London's largest leisure park, Lee Valley has a variety of self-guided walks, in addition to its many other activities and facilities.

I. Fishers Green

There are two self-guided walks to follow here, taking you around a series of large lakes, meadows and woodland. Starting points along the walk include Cadmore Lane, Windmill Lane, Highbridge Street, Abbeyview and Crooked Mile. Phone 01992 893345 for information leaflets.

2. River Lea Navigation Towpath

The towpath runs almost the full length of the valley.

3. Bowyers Water Circular Walks
From Hooks Marsh car park
There are several footpaths across Waltham Marsh (leading to Waltham Hall) to follow. A leaflet is available from the Countryside Centre (see below).

For more details on all these walks and to find out about other outdoor activities and events, contact or visit the Lee Valley Countryside Centre, Abbey Farmhouse, Crooked Mile, Waltham Abbey, Essex EN9 1QX (01992 713838).

London Silver Jubilee Walkway
This circular 19-kilometre (12-mile) walk was created for the Queen's Silver Jubilee in 1977. It starts at Leicester Square, passes through Westminster and over Lambeth Bridge, then along the south bank to Tower Bridge and back through the City, Fleet Street, Holborn and Covent Garden. The route is marked by 400 large discs set in the pavement and is easy to follow.

Parkland Walk
Walk along the railway line that used to connect Finsbury Park Station and Alexandra Palace, running from Finsbury Park through Queen's and Highgate Woods to Muswell Hill. It is also an important local nature reserve where 32 per cent of Britain's breeding butterfly species can be found and fifty-three species of bird, as well as 233 different kinds of flowering plants.
Start: Oxford Road, N4 or Finsbury Park
Ө/BR Finsbury Park
❑ 4, 19, 29, 106, 153, 236, 253, 259, 279

Finish: Muswell Hill
Ө Highgate
BR Alexandra Park
❑ W7, 43, X43, 102, 134, 144, 234, 299

Thames Path
The Thames Path is the newest National Trail in England and runs from the Thames Barrier in Woolwich to the river's source at Kemble in Gloucestershire. Managed by the Countryside Commission, this unique path is the only long-distance route in Britain to follow a river almost throughout its entire length and to pass through major towns and cities.

River Cray and River Shuttle Walks
Bexley
There is a fascinating, marked 16-kilometre (10-mile) river walk along the River Cray and through the ancient woodland at North Cray Woods. Starting in Foots Cray Meadows off Rectory Lane in Bexley, it follows the river through North Cray to Hall Place at Bexley, where the Cray is joined by its tributary, the Shuttle. From Hall Place, they flow down through Crayford and join the River Darent and then the Thames.

Two leaflets are available covering both the Shuttle and Cray river walks from Bexley Planning Department, Wyncham House, 207 Longlands Road, Sidcup, Kent DA15 7JH.
BR Bexley, Crayford, Eltham, Erith, Slade Green

Wandle Trail

This 19-kilometre (12-mile) walk takes you through parkland and industrial wasteland, urban streets and garden suburbs from just north of Armoury Way in Wandsworth to Beddington Park in Croydon; many years ago it was fields and watercress beds. For details of the trail, contact the Wandle Industrial Museum, The Vestry Hall, London Road, Mitcham, Surrey CR4 9UJ (tel: 0181 648 0127), or the Ramblers' Association, 105 Wandsworth Road, London SW8 2XX (tel: 0171 582 6878).
BR Putney, Wandsworth Town
❑ 151, 255, 400, 407, 408, 726

SOCIETY-RUN WALKS

Several conservation, architecture and arts societies run guided walks for members in and around London. The guides are excellent, the prices cheap and the walks often include entry to places usually closed to the general public. Societies which run these walks include the National Art Collections Fund (tel: 0171 821 0404) and the Ancient Monuments Society (tel: 0171 236 3934) and conservation groups, such as the Heath and Old Hampstead Society (tel: 0171 722 9512). Contact them directly for more information on membership.
££

CHARITY WALKS

Keep an eye out for posters advertising charity walks in the local and national press. They are becoming a popular way to raise money and, as they are usually a relaxed affair with the emphasis on fun, the whole family can join in.

GUIDED WALKS

There are several companies which provide a wide range of walking tours through London. The length of the walks varies from a couple of hours to a whole day, and they are geared to suit all different ages. They are a great way to meet people and to learn more about parts of London you are usually too busy to notice. To go on a walk, meet your guide and fellow walkers just outside the designated meeting place at the stated time. Most walks last about two hours and end near Underground stations. There is often no need to book and walks take place whatever the weather.

Cockney Walk

Cockney Museum, 32 Anworth Close, Woodford Green, Essex (0181 504 9159)
These walks are designed to show visitors some of the most interesting and

colourful parts of the East End and can be adapted to suit particular interests, such as the docks or the traditional Jewish areas.
££

Citisights

The Old Operating Theatre Museum, 9a St Thomas's Street SE1 9RT (0171 357 0090; fax: 0171 837 6951)
The most popular walk run by Citisights is the London Story, which starts at the Museum of London and explores the City, covering its history from ancient myth to the modern money markets. Other walks include the Secret City, the London of Dickens and Shakespeare, Legal London and Ancient Inns and Taverns.
££ (discounts for students, concessions and OAPs)

Discovering London

11 Pennyfields, Warley, Brentwood, Essex (01277 213704)
Send for the summer or winter programme, enclosing a stamped-addressed envelope. No booking needed. Outdoor tours include strolls around Sherlock Holmes's London, Historic Westminster, the Charm of Chelsea and lots more.
££

Guided Walks in Richmond, Twickenham and Kew

Tourist Information Centre, Old Town Hall, Whittaker Avenue, Richmond, Surrey TW9 1SX (0181 940 9125)
The Society of Voluntary Guides runs three different, regular walks in this area, appealing not only to visitors but to locals too. Private walks for groups are also available.
££ (discounts for concessions)

Historical Tours

John Muffty, 3 Florence Road, South Croydon, Surrey CR2 0PQ (0181 668 4019; fax: 0181 760 9664)
Walks include The London of Dickens and Shakespeare, a Historic Pub Walk in Mayfair and Chelsea, the Jack the Ripper Murder Trail, a walk in the footsteps of Sherlock Holmes and a Ghost Pub Walk.
££ (discounts for children and OAPs; children under fourteen enter free when accompanied by an adult)

London (Japanese) Walking Tours

39 Burrard Road, West Hampstead NW6 1DA (0171 266 4729; fax: 0171 433 1184)
This programme of walks led by Japanese-speaking guides takes you from Chelsea

to Docklands and Greenwich, by way of a trip through Sherlock Holmes's Case Book and Shakespeare and Dickens's London. There is also a selection of special walks which end either with afternoon tea or a visit to the pub (book 48 hours in advance).
££

Original Ghost Walks
41 Spelman Street, Spitalfields, E1 5LQ (0171 247 5604)
Regular walks 'visiting' the Ghosts of London start from outside the Blackfriars Pub, White Lion Street, Blackfriars at 9.00 p.m., while for the less ghoulish there is a good choice of daytime walks.
££ (discounts for concessions)

Original London Walks
PO Box 1708, NW6 1PQ (0171 624 3978; fax same number)
London's longest established walking tour agency boasts an impressive list of tour guides and an interesting and wide selection of walks. These include the London of Shakespeare and Dickens, Jack the Ripper Haunts, the Old Jewish Quarter, Legal London, the Beatles' Magical Mystery Tour and Historic Greenwich.
££ (discounts for students and OAPs; children under fifteen go free if accompanied by an adult. If you want to go on several walks, ask for a Discount Walkabout Ticket – they are excellent value for money)

Thameside Ventures
6 Manor Way, Abbey Wood, SE2 4PL (0181 317 7722)
Fred Sage, who has worked as a stevedore and seaman in London's old docks, gives a personal insight to the history of the Thames.
££

Tour Guides International
2 Bridge Street, Westminster, SW1A 2JR (0171 839 2498; fax: 0171 839 5314)
Tour Guides differ from the other groups already mentioned as they specialize in the planning of unusual London walks. They have a membership of 200 registered tourist board (blue badge) guides who, between them, have enormous expertise and can cater for any demand. Among the walks offered are In the Steps of Princess Diana, Jack the Ripper (still the most popular), Government and Democracy, Royal Westminster, Soho and the Sixties and Upstairs Downstairs in Belgravia. Book ahead for special requests.
££

Overleaf: Kenwood House Gardens

NATURALISTS'
LONDON

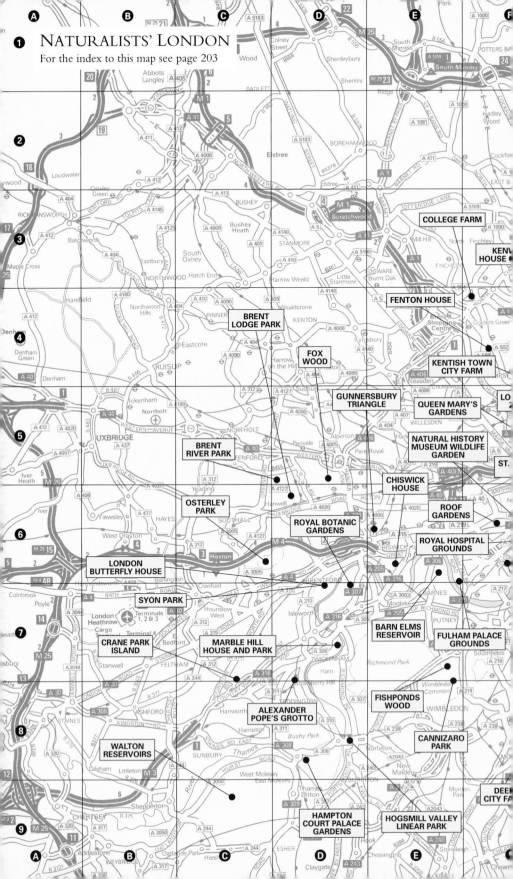

NATURALISTS' LONDON
For the index to this map see page 203

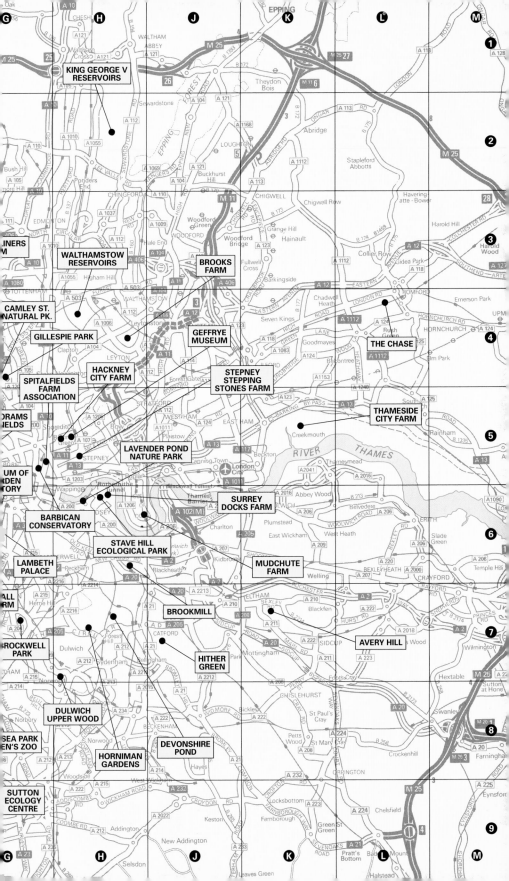

5

BIRDS, FLOWERS AND WILDLIFE

CENTRAL LONDON does not immediately spring to mind as a wildlife haven, but, nevertheless, it is home to a surprisingly wide range of plant and animal life. For some time now foxes have been moving into urban areas, while in parks you will see squirrels and wood pigeons, along with the occasional badger.

Birds play an important role in London wildlife, and have adapted remarkably easily to inner-city life, often nesting above busy roads, untroubled by the noise and pollution around them. Further out large open spaces such as Hampstead Heath and Epping Forest maintain a healthy population of birds too, as does every suburban garden, and in certain places you might be lucky enough to spot a kestrel or even a tawny owl.

The future of London's wildlife is a vital issue and conservation groups such as the London Wildlife Trust, the British Trust for Conservation Volunteers, the Royal Society for the Protection of Birds, British Waterways and the London Natural History Society are working hard to ensure that our open spaces are preserved by promoting public awareness of the environment.

Volunteers are always welcome to help with all types of conservation projects; these can vary from transforming derelict areas into a natural wildlife habitat, to standing knee-deep in water to clear an overgrown pond, or to counting the number and variety of birds in your garden.

NATURE RESERVES

As part of its work, the London Wildlife Trust has set up and now manages fifty-two nature reserves across Greater London. The most interesting are listed below, along with London's other main nature reserves.

Abney Park Cemetery
Bouverie Road, Stoke Newington, N16 (0171 249 8928)
A Victorian cemetery with woodland, thick undergrowth and, in the spring, a delightful carpet of bluebells. The entrance is on Stoke Newington Church Street.
⊖ Manor House
BR Stoke Newington
❏ 67, 73, 76, 106, 149, 243, 243A
Open: daily, 9.00 a.m.–5.00 p.m.

Boston Manor Nature Trail

Boston Manor Road, Boston Gardens, Brentford, Middlesex TW8 (0181 556 1929)
A trail runs from the lake at Boston Manor Park through the wood, across the River Brent, under the M4 and on to Clitheroes Island. Then it passes past the lock gates and on to the Grand Union Canal towpath. Nature trail leaflet available.
⊖ Boston Manor
❑ E8
Open: daily

Brent River Park

Brentford, W7 (0181 566 1929 (Ranger)
See also page 76
This chain of green spaces stretches along the banks of the River Brent, with woodland walks, blackberries and the unusual canal 'staircase' of Hanwell's flight of locks.

Part of the chain is a 1.2-hectare (3-acre) ancient woodland, Longwood, particularly interesting for birds and wild flowers, with a clean stream. There is a board walk to help access over parts of the wet woodland.

Details of five interesting circular walks in a useful guide are available from Brent River Park Environmental Centre (also displays of local wildlife, natural history and conservation issues), based at Brent Lodge Park, Church Road, W7.
⊖ Perivale
BR Hanwell, South Greenford
❑ E1, E3
Open: park, daily; *Environmental Centre,* please phone for details

Brookmill

Brookmill Road, Lewisham, SE8 (0181 778 8212/659 2303)
Located on an old railway embankment, the reserve is a mixture of woodland and meadow. The main feature is a small pond which provides a breeding place for frogs and aquatic invertebrates, while the scrubland area provides food for birds and the occasional fox. Along the north side of the site conditions are suitable for woodland glade flowers such as bluebells and herb Robert. Just inside the gate an area has been planted with cornfield annuals, such as poppies and corncockle.
⊖/**BR** New Cross
❑ 47, 225
Open: daily

Camley Street Natural Park

Camley Street, King's Cross, NW1 (0171 278 6612: London Wildlife Trust)
An innovative and internationally acclaimed natural park on the banks of the Regent's Canal, Camley Street has been painstakingly created to provide a natural environment for birds, bees, butterflies, frogs and toads, as well as for a rich variety of plant life. There is also a visitors' centre/classroom well stocked with information leaflets.
Θ/**BR** King's Cross
❏ 46, 214
Open: Monday–Thursday, 9.30 a.m.–5.00 p.m.; Friday, closed; Saturday–Sunday, 11.00 a.m.–5.00 p.m.

The Chase

Dagenham Road and Upper Rainham Road, Romford, Essex RM7 (0171 278 6612: London Wildlife Trust)
The London Wildlife Trust's largest reserve in London combines grassland with small ponds and large lakes created when gravel pits were flooded. Originally ancient grazing marshes, today the Chase is still grazed by horses, as well as providing a habitat for a variety of wildlife, trees and plants. Of particular interest are rare plants such as the marshy cudweed and grassland ground-nesting birds, and, in the larger pools, there are newts, frogs and waterfowl. See also page 35.
Θ Dagenham East
BR Romford
❏ 174, 252
Open: daily

Crane Park Island

via Crane Park, Ellerman Avenue, Twickenham, Middlesex TW2 (0171 278 6612: London Wildlife Trust)
Surrounded by the beautiful River Crane, this artificial island is a mosaic of woodland, scrub and meadow. Its unusual history began in 1776 when the island was created to provide water for a gunpowder mill. When the mill closed, in 1926, the island developed into a woodland and all that is left of its industrial past is the imposing Shot Tower nearby. In the centre of the island is the millpond, which supports amphibians, grasses, willow and nettles and butterflies.
BR Whitton
❏ 110, 111
Open: daily

Devonshire Pond

Between 168 and 174 Devonshire Road, Forest Hill, SE23 (0181 858 6106)
The woodland is dominated by hawthorn and sycamore, with some large oak and ash trees too. These trees provide a habitat for grey squirrels and birds, such as jays, wood pigeons, willow warblers and blackcaps. Speckled butterflies are common too. Foxes can occasionally be seen in the scrub area, while the grassland is home to grasshoppers, eight species of ant, particularly the yellow ant, and to plants such as wild carrot, black medick and cowslip.
BR Forest Hill
❏ 122, 176, 185, 194, 312
Open: 2.00 p.m.–4.00 p.m. every Saturday; on weekdays by arrangement

Duck Wood

Sheffield Drive, Harold Hill, Essex RM3 (0171 278 6612: London Wildlife Trust)
An ancient hornbeam woodland which is noted for carpets of bluebells and wood anemones. Additional features include woodland birds and a series of ten ponds, but, unfortunately, no resident ducks as yet.
BR Harold Wood
❏ 246, 256, 294, 296
Open: daily

Dulwich Upper Wood

Farquhar Road, Dulwich, SE19 (0171 237 9165)
Dulwich Upper Wood is close to the site of the old Crystal Palace and is a 2-hectare (5-acre) remnant of the Great North Wood which once stretched from New Cross to Croydon. The wood grew up from the abandoned gardens of old Victorian houses (now demolished) and a small core of ancient woodland which had survived in the area. Many of the trees are sycamore, but there are also old oak, ash, yew and chestnut trees.

   Special features include a herb garden and a network of nature trails, some of which are suitable for wheelchairs.
BR Gypsy Hill
❏ 2, 3, 63, 122, 137A, 157, 202, 227, 249, 306, 322, 352, 358, 450
Open: daily

Fishponds Wood

Off Beverley Meads, Wimbledon Common, Wimbledon, SW20 (0171 278 6612: London Wildlife Trust)
Fishponds Wood, lying between Beverley Brook and Beverley Meads, is possibly the most interesting part of Wimbledon Common to naturalists. Here you will find trees such as hazel, oak, birch and holly, with wetland plants near the ponds, such as moss. The varied terrain throughout the Common provides suitable habitats for various animals such as foxes, rabbits and badgers.
Θ/**BR** Wimbledon
❏ 57
Open: daily

Fox Wood

Fox Lane, off Sandal Road, Ealing, W5 (0171 278 6612: London Wildlife Trust)
This small nature reserve is situated on part of a former reservoir – the rest is now playing fields. Comprising woodland bordered by two small wildflower meadows, it is home to over sixty species of birds, including tawny owls and chiffchaffs, and butterflies such as the speckled brown. Plants include bluebells in spring and mushrooms in autumn, while the woodland is dominated by oak, sycamore, holly and bramble.

⊖ Hanger Lane
❑ 83, 112
Open: daily

Gillespie Park

Gillespie Road, Highbury, N5 (0171 354 5413)
A community wildlife park close to the football ground at Arsenal and based on railway sidings. It is a small woodland area complete with a pond and is home to eighty-three species of bird, including various finches, tits and thrushes. There are twenty-two recorded breeds of butterflies, such as the speckled wood, small heath and small tortoiseshell, as well as frogs, newts, toads and sticklebacks in the ponds. Disabled access is from St Thomas Road.

⊖ Arsenal
❑ 4, 19, 236
Open: 8 a.m.–dusk daily, except when Arsenal is playing at home

Grand Union Canal (North Bank)

Entrance on Ladbroke Grove, Kensal Green, W10 (0171 278 6612: London Wildlife Trust)
Part of the valuable inner-city green corridor, this narrow canal bank provides space for water birds and interesting water plants such as pondweed and rushes.

⊖.BR Kensal Green
❑ 7, 23, 52, 295, 302
Open: daily

Gunnersbury Triangle

Bollo Lane, Chiswick, W3 (0181 747 3881: Warden)
A woodland with tall silver birches, hidden ponds and marshy areas gives a sense of wilderness to this area of abandoned railway land. In 1983 local residents successfully fought to save the Triangle from development and it is now managed as a nature reserve by the London Wildlife Trust. There is a pond which attracts birds such as the sedge warbler and the redpoll, while water plants include the celery-laced buttercup and the bulrush.

⊖ Chiswick Park
❑ H40
Open: Monday–Friday, 8.30 a.m.–4.30 p.m.; Sunday 2.00 p.m.–4.30 p.m.

Ham Lands Nature Reserve

Riverside Drive, Ham, Surrey TW10 (0181 940 8351: Conservation Officer)
Some 80 hectares (200 acres) of meadowland is still grazed by cows, and there is also some recent woodland along the east bank of the Thames. Excellent for fishing, riding, walking and picnics.
⊖/BR Richmond (then 10 minutes' walk along the river)
❑ 371
Open: daily

Hither Green

Between Hose Avenue and Baring Road, Hither Green, SE12 (0181 778 8212/659 2303)
This reserve comprises 2.5 hectares (6 acres) of varied wildlife habitat. In an area of scrub there is a predominance of bramble, along with buttercups, ragwort and hogweed. There is also an old plum orchard, where bullfinches are found in spring, and a pond which supports frogs and other amphibians.

A wooded area contains seventeen species of tree, such as horse chestnut, oak, ash, sycamore and willow. Here you will see blackbirds, robins, magpies and the occasional green woodpecker, while on sunny days you might find slowworms or common lizards on the grassy area.
BR Hither Green, Lee
❑ 261
Open: daily

Hogsmill Valley Linear Park

Kingston Town Centre to Ashtead Common (0181 546 2121: London Wildlife Trust)
A riverside walkway along the Hogsmill River and Bonesgate Stream stretches from Kingston town centre in the north, through former meadowland and woodland, via Horton Country Park, to the Green Belt in the south. The area is still being regenerated by the London Wildlife Trust to improve the woodland structure, but you can already find foxes, rabbits and even water voles.
BR Ashtead, Kingston
❑ K1, K2, K4, K5, K9, K10, 57, 65, 71, 85, 111, 131, 213, 216, 218, 281, 285, 371, 406, 411, 431, 437, 440, 451, 461, 465, 479, 501, 511, 513, 527, 561, 572, 582, 592, 726, 727
Open: daily

Horsenden Hill

Off Horsenden Lane North, Greenford, Middlesex UB6 (0181 903 3945: Countryside Ranger)
See page 77
An ancient rural area, near the northern boundary of Ealing, this hill gives magnificent views across London. The most interesting feature is the varied grassland, which includes rye grass, sweet vernal grass and Timothy grass.
⊖ Greenford, Perivale, Sudbury Town
BR Greenford
❑ H17, 92, 187
Open: daily

Ickenham Marsh

Footpath from junction of Glebe Avenue and Austin's Lane, Ickenham, Middlesex UB10 (0171 278 6612: London Wildlife Trust)
Open oak woodland with scattered scrub next to damp meadows and marsh bordering the Yeading Brook. This varied habitat supports a wealth of plants and trees, such as hawthorn, bramble and holly, while wildlife includes frogs, newts, foxes and squirrels.
⊖ Ickenham
❏ U1, U10
Open: daily

Kidbrooke Green

Between Rochester Way, Nelson Mandela Road and Rochester Way Relief Road, Blackheath, SE3 (0171 278 6612: London Wildlife Trust)
An interesting wetland reserve, Kidbrooke Green is one of the few remaining areas of ancient marshland which once ran along the length of the Kidbrooke. It is home to breeding frogs, toads and newts, as well as birds such as the snipe, fieldfare and redwing.
BR Kidbrooke
❏ B16
Open: daily

Lavender Pond Nature Park

Off Rotherhithe Street, Rotherhithe, SE16 (0171 232 0498)
Lavender Pond Nature Park was created in 1981 in the northern part of the former Surrey Commercial Docks. Close to the park is the Pumphouse, an old pumping station which now houses an Environmental Studies Centre and the Rotherhithe Heritage Museum.

The water in Lavender Pond is fresh and clear and supports a great variety of animals and plants, including dragonflies and water skaters. Water birds, such as moorhens, mallards and even swans, visit the pond as its edges provide a protected nesting place.
⊖ Rotherhithe
❏ P11, P13, 225
Open: most weekdays and some weekends; please phone for details

❖

London Wildlife Garden Centre
28 Marsden Road, Dulwich, SE15 (0171 252 9186: London Wildlife Trust)
This centre is full of ideas for transforming your garden into a haven for wildlife, with many wild flowers and trees available for purchase, plus demonstration areas and a visitors' centre.
BR East Dulwich
❑ P13, S13, 37, 40, 176, 185, 484
Open: Tuesday, Wednesday, Thursday, Sunday, 11.00 a.m.– 4.00 p.m.

Natural History Wildlife Garden
Natural History Museum, Cromwell Road, South Kensington, SW7 (0171 938 8000)
Situated in the south-western corner of the museum's grounds, the new Wildlife Garden, covering roughly 0.5 hectare (1 acre) in area, represents a range of British plant and wildlife habitats, including a chalk meadow, bluebell woods, three ponds and a waterfall.

Its primary purpose is as an educational tool for children, as well as offering excellent opportunities for scientific research, especially in the field of urban ecology.
⊖ South Kensington
❑ C1, 14, 45A, 49, 70, 74
Open: daily, 10.00 a.m.–5.30 p.m.

Rowley Green Common
Rowley Lane, Barnet, Hertfordshire EN4 (0171 278 6612: London Wildlife Trust)
The bog is the main feature here – one of only a few sphagnum bogs in London. It provides a habitat for the lesser spearwort and other wetland plants. There is also woodland where bats have been seen, as well as mice, voles and foxes.
⊖ Cockfosters
BR New Barnet
❑ 107
Open: daily

Stave Hill Ecological Park
Timber Pond Road, Rotherhithe, SE16 (0171 237 9175)
Stave Hill has become a haven for butterflies, with over twenty species visiting this rich mosaic of wild flowers, woodland and shrub. In recognition of this diversity, the park has been designated Britain's first urban butterfly sanctuary, forming part of a wider campaign by Butterfly Conservation – a national group striving to redress the decline in Britain's butterfly population. New projects include an orchard, fungi garden, school nature plots and a hop garden.
⊖ Rotherhithe
❑ P11, P13, 225
Open: daily

Sutton Ecology Centre
Old Rectory, Festival Walk, Carshalton, Surrey (0181 773 4018)
Set in a pretty, rural location in Carshalton, with a beautiful Queen Anne House as its headquarters, this is an attractive setting for an informative and attractive

ecology centre. Pond, marshes, woods, wild flower meadows and orchards are all home to ducks, herons, dragonflies and kingfishers in this wildlife haven.
BR Carshalton
❑ 127, 157, 408, 726
Open: centre Monday–Saturday, 10.00 a.m.– 4.00 p.m.; *grounds* daily, dawn– dusk

Sydenham Hill Wood

Crescent Wood Road, off Sydenham Hill, Sydenham, SE26 (0171 278 6612: London Wildlife Trust)
A rich mix of ancient and recent woodland, home to woodpeckers and warblers, bluebells and even bamboo!
BR Forest Hill, Sydenham Hill
❑ 63, 122, 176, 185, 312
Open: daily

Ten Acre Wood

Entrance at east end of Charville Lane North, Hayes, Middlesex UB4 (0171 278 6612: London Wildlife Trust)
An oak woodland surrounded by flower-rich meadows and scrub adjoining Yeading Brook. Look out for buttercups, willow herbs and cow parsley.
⊖ Ickenham
❑ 195, 207A
Open: daily

Canal Wildlife

Since they were first built, London's canals have acquired many plants and animals and today they provide a wonderful variety of wildlife habitats. Some breeds have survived from when the canals were first built and others have come in from the countryside or from parks and gardens within London. They have been able to use the canals as a natural highway for migration and dispersal, through what would otherwise be hostile territory. This is why rural plants such as skullcap and the great water dock have been able reach London.

Another important factor was the enormous number of boats transporting goods such as grain that used the canal until recently. With every accidental spillage, a few grains would survive – this is how canary grass and cultivated flax arrived.

The towpaths and banks are thriving wildlife habitats too, supporting grassland, scrub and trees. Canal walls and the shallow edges of canals are home to species typical of marshlands, while the canals themselves are able to support water plants, invertebrates and fish.

Please help to conserve this environment. Never pick wild flowers or try to transplant them to your home; they are unlikely to survive and you will prevent other visitors enjoying them.

❖

Tump 53

Entrance on Bentham Road, Thamesmead, SE28 (0171 278 6612: London Wildlife Trust)
Part of the old Woolwich Arsenal, Tump 53 was used as an ammunition store in the late nineteenth century and now provides open water, reedbeds, meadow and scrub.
BR Abbey Wood
❏ 229, 244, 272, 401
Open: daily

Wilderness Island

Entrance on corner of Mill Lane and Strawberry Lane, Sutton (0171 278 6612: London Wildlife Trust)
An island in the River Wandle with a mixed habitat of ponds, sedge bed, meadow and woodland, with a good nature trail.
BR Carshalton
❏ 127, 157, 408, 726
Open: daily

Yeading Brook Meadows

Off Kinshill Avenue, Opp. Attlee Road, Greenford, Middlesex UB6 (0181 903 3945: Countryside Ranger)
The open damp meadows along the Yeading Brook contain over 100 kinds of wild flower, many of them rare, such as cowslips.
⊖ Hillingdon, Ickenham
❏ E9, 90, 140
Open: daily

BIRD-WATCHING

Reservoirs are excellent places to find more unusual birds and are important wildlife areas. You will need a permit to visit them. Details are given below, along with information on London's main bird-watching sites.

LONDON'S TOP BIRD-WATCHING SITES

Barn Elms Reservoir

Merthyr Terrace, off Castelnau, Barnes, SW13 (01734 593363: Recreation Manager)
This is an excellent bird-watching location, within easy reach of central London. Over 200 different types of bird have been recorded, including thirty-one species of wildfowl, thirty-three species of wader and two species of gull and tern. Shovelers and tufted ducks

Tips for Identifying Birds

Bird-watching is great fun, but remember that it does takes practice to be able to identify what you see. If you are a beginner, one of the best ways to start is to take a field guide, notebook and pencil with you when you go for a walk.

When you see a bird you do not recognize, first compare it with birds you already know. Ask yourself questions such as, is it smaller than a pigeon? or, is it the same colour as a sparrow? Make notes about shape, the type of legs, bill and wings and if there are any unusual markings or features.

Another point to note is location, as a bird's habitat will also help identify it. Check all your information with your bird guide and hopefully you will be able to identify it.

It is well worth joining the Royal Society for the Protection of Birds (RSPB) if you are interested in bird-watching and bird conservation. The RSPB has an active youth section too; children can join the Young Ornithologists' Society, which holds regular events and activities.

also come here in winter. Many gulls roost here during the winter too, while spring and autumn bring migrants such as waders, terns, gulls, wagtails, warblers and swifts.

ϴ Hammersmith

❑ 9, 9A, 33, R69, 72

Open: daily, 7.30 a.m.–sunset

££ (for permits)

Kempton Park West

Sunbury Way, Hanworth, Middlesex TW13 (01734 593363: Recreation Manager)
Since this reservoir was drained, the resulting marshy grassland, reedbeds and willow scrub have provided temporary habitats for warblers and wildfowl such as teals.

BR Sunbury

❑ H25, 290

Open: Monday–Wednesday, 7.30 a.m.–4.30 p.m.; Thursday–Friday, 7.30 a.m.–3.30 p.m.

££ (for permits)

King George V Reservoirs

Lea Valley Road, Chingford, E4 (0181 808 1527: Gatehouse)
A Site of Special Scientific Interest, this is an area of national importance for waterfowl, with large numbers of moulting tufted duck in late summer and goosanders, goldeneyes and black-necked grebes in the winter. Terns, little gulls, pipits, wagtails and buntings, plus a wide selection of waders, can also be seen.

BR Brimsdown, Ponders End

❑ 191, 313

Open: daily, except 25 and 26 December, 7.30 a.m.–1 hour after sunset

££ (for permits)

Walthamstow Reservoirs

Ferry Lane, Tottenham, N17 (0181 808 1527: information)
A Site of Special Scientific Interest, the main features are the large heronries on the reservoir's small islands and a cormorant roost. Rarities include sabine gulls, little egrets and green-winged teals.
BR Blackhorse Road, Tottenham Hale
❑ W4, 41, 123, 230
Open: daily, except 25 and 26 December, 7.00 a.m.–1 hour after sunset
££ (for permits)

Walton Reservoirs

Hurst Road, Walton-on-Thames, Surrey KT12 and Hersham Road, Sunbury, Upper Haliford, Surrey KT12 (01734 593363: Recreation Manager)
These reservoirs are noted for the wintering flocks of diving ducks, such as the goldeneye, as well as for shovelers, gadwalls, teals and wigeons. Late summer brings the moulting tufted duck, while other birds include the red-breasted merganser. A key can be obtained from the gatehouse at Walton.
BR Sunbury, Walton-on-Thames
❑ 131, 431, 718
Open: Monday–Thursday, 7.00 a.m.–5.00 p.m., Friday, 7.00 a.m.–1.30 p.m.
££ (for permits)

6
CITY FARMS, ZOOS AND ANIMAL ENCLOSURES

CITY FARMS

A LTHOUGH London's first show farm, College Farm in Finchley, was established in the 1880s, in the past decade city farms have sprung up all over London, many in some of the most deprived areas of the East End, where they have become a popular feature with the local communities. Although every farm usually has the same selection of animals – chickens, goats, geese, rabbits and guinea pigs seem the most popular – they each have their own unique atmosphere and charm. The most noticeable common feature is the enthusiasm of the staff for their particular farm, which passes down to volunteers. Most farms encourage children of all ages to join in, but they must be committed to a long-term involvement and most children are aged eight or over.

Brooks Farm
Skeltons Lane Park, Leyton, E10 (0181 539 4278)
Animals here include a Vietnamese pot-bellied pig, goats, sheep, ducks, geese, rabbits, chickens and doves. The farm also holds craft demonstrations and activity weekends. Please phone for details. Facilities include a snack bar, a picnic area, a nappy-changing area, a play area for under-sixes and an adventure playground for under-thirteens.
Θ/**BR** Leyton Midland Road
❑ 69, 97
Open: Wednesday–Sunday, 10.30 a.m.–5.30 p.m.

College Farm
45 Fitzalan Road, Finchley, N3 (0181 349 0690)
Originally set up as the 'Showplace of the Dairy Industry' in 1883, this 4-hectare (10-acre) farm was the first working farm in Britain to become a tourist attraction. It is now a conservation area – the farm buildings are Grade II listed – with cows,
pigs, shire horses, ponies, donkeys, rabbits, sheep, chickens and Highland cattle.
Facilities include a picture gallery and a visitors' centre and shop selling animal feed, pet food and saddlery. There is a tea room at weekends and on the first Sunday

afternoon of every month there is a Country Fête from 2.00 p.m. until 6.00 p.m.
⊖/BR Finchley Central
❏ 82, 143, 260, 326
Open: daily, 10.00 a.m.–6.00 p.m.
£

Crystal Palace Urban Farmyard
Crystal Palace Park Road, SE20 (0181 778 7148)
See also page 30
A city farm where you will find goats, pigs, shire horses and cows, as well as a variety of caged birds.
BR Crystal Palace
❏ 2, 3, 63, 122, 137A, 157, 202, 227, 249, 306, 322, 352, 358, 450
Open: daily, 11.00 a.m.–5.00 p.m.
££

Deen City Farm
39 Windsor Avenue, Merton Abbey, SW19 (0181 543 5300)
The farm has been open since 1980 and is home to sheep, pigs, goats, rabbits, chickens, guinea fowl, horses, ponies and bees. Spinning, weaving and dyeing classes for adults are also held here. Please phone for details.

Facilities include a farm shop, selling eggs, goat's milk, honey and yoghurt, herbs and vegetables; a registered riding school and a restaurant as well as a visitors' centre.
⊖ Colliers Wood, South Wimbledon
❏ 200
Open: daily 9.00 a.m.– 4.00 p.m.

Freightliners Farm
Paradise Park, Sheringham Road, Holloway, N7 (0171 609 0467)
A 1-hectare (2½-acre) working farm with cows, sheep, pigs, goats, geese, turkeys, chickens and ducks. There is also a classroom for educational projects (phone for details), a nursery and a budding wildlife garden. Volunteers are welcome.

Facilities include a visitors' centre and a farm shop selling a variety of produce, including manure!
⊖ Highbury & Islington, Holloway Road
❏ 43, 153, 271, 279
Open: Tuesday–Sunday 9.00 a.m.–5.00 p.m.

Hackney City Farm
1a Goldsmiths Row, E2 (0171 729 6381)
A wonderfully converted brewery complete with a cobbled yard forms the centrepiece of this farm in the heart of the East End. Meet goats, sheep, chickens, turkeys, pigs, ducks, rabbits, guinea pigs and bees. There is also a small orchard, an ecological area and wildlife pond, a vegetable plot and a herb garden. You can learn all sorts of skills here too, including beekeeping, animal feeding, gardening, spinning, weaving and pottery, and there are special

activities for children, the elderly and the handicapped.

Facilities include a café and a visitors' centre.

⊖ Bethnal Green
BR Cambridge Heath
❏ 26, 48, 55

Open: café Tuesday–Friday, 10.00 a.m.–4.30 p.m.; Saturday and Sunday, 10.00 a.m. –12 a.m.; *farm* Tuesday–Sunday, 10.00 a.m.–4.30 p.m.

Kentish Town City Farm
Cressfield Close, Kentish Town, NW5 (0171 482 2861)
One of London's oldest city farms, established in 1973, it has a friendly, easy-going atmosphere, making it particularly popular with children. As well as all the usual farm animals, such as cows, pigs and goats, there is a pensioners' garden, a children's garden and a developing nature area. Small children and children with special needs can learn to ride here.
⊖ Kentish Town
❏ C11, C12, 24, 46
Open: Tuesday–Sunday 9.00 a.m.–6.00 p.m.

Mudchute Farm
Pier Street, Millwall, E14 (0171 515 5901)
Mudchute Urban Park and Farm, to give it its full name, was created in the last century when silt from the construction of surrounding docks was dumped and a natural wilderness grew up. For decades this hidden natural wilderness remained an East End secret, until 1977, when the Mudchute Association was formed to preserve and develop the area and farm animals were introduced.

It is now a working farm and animal attractions include horses and ponies, sheep, cattle, goats, pigs, chickens, ducks, geese, rabbits, guinea pigs and even a llama. There is a registered riding school here, and it is among the cheapest in London.
DLR Mudchute (Monday–Friday, 5.30 a.m.–12.00 a.m.)
❏ D7, D8, D9
Open: daily, 8.30 a.m.–5.00 p.m.

Newham City Farm
King George Avenue, Plaistow, E16 (0171 476 1170)
An immaculate farm just a stone's throw from London's City Airport, the main feature here is the 'farm club', through which volunteers can muck in with all sorts of farm work. There is also a fascinating collection of llamas and wallabies, as well as sheep, cows, geese, ducks, hamsters, ferrets and guinea pigs.
DLR City Airport, Silvertown (Monday–Friday, 5.30 a.m.–12.00 a.m.)
❏ X15, 262, 276, 300
Open: Tuesday–Sunday 10.00 a.m.–5.00 p.m.

Spitalfields Farm Association
Weaver Street, Spitalfields, E1 (0171 247 8762)
The warm welcome and lively atmosphere on this farm, built on BR wasteland in the heart of the East End, makes Spitalfields one of the most appealing farms

in London. The staff encourage a hands-on approach for visitors, with the emphasis on training and education. There are horticultural training schemes for school leavers, adult education classes, horse and cart tours and other activities for the young and the old.

There are goats, hens, horses, rabbits ducks and guinea pigs here and facilities include a café and a visitors' centre.

⊖ Shoreditch, Whitechapel

❑ 5, 8, 22A, 22B, 26, 35, 43, 47, 48, 55, 67, 78, 149, 243, 243A, 505

Open: Tuesday–Sunday, 9.30 a.m.–5.30 p.m.

Stepney Stepping Stones Farm

Corner of Stepney Way and Stepney High Street, Stepney, E1 (0171 790 8204)

Animals here include ducks, hens, sheep, rabbits, guinea pigs, quails, cows, goats and pigs. There is also a fully equipped classroom with a qualified teacher and a wildlife area.

Facilities include a café (only open at weekends), a visitors' centre and spinning and weaving classes.

⊖ Whitechapel

DLR Limehouse (Monday–Friday, 5.30 a.m.–12.00 a.m.)

❑ 25, 106, 253

Open: Tuesday–Saturday, 9.30 a.m.–6.00 p.m. (closed 1.00 p.m.–2.00 p.m.)

Surrey Docks Farm

South Wharf, Off Salter Road at end of Rotherhithe Street, Surrey Docks, SE16 (0171 231 1010)

There are goats, geese, ducks, chickens, donkeys and bees here, and facilities include a visitors' centre.

⊖ Rotherhithe

❑ P11, 225

Open: Tuesday–Sunday, 10.00 a.m.–5.00 p.m. (closed 1.00 p.m.–2.00 p.m. weekends)

Kentish Town City Farm

❖

City Farms by Tube

Nearest stations: Kentish Town for Grafton Road,
Aldgate East or Shoreditch for Pedley Street,
Surrey Quays for Rotherhithe Street,
Hatton Cross for Faggs Road,
Vauxhall for Tyers Street

City Farms by Lizzie Riches
A new work of art commissioned by London Underground

Art on the Underground

Thameside City Farm

40 Thames Road, Barking, Essex IG11 (0181 594 8449)
Lying in the middle of a barren industrial estate in east London is a small haven for farm animals, wildlife and children. Much hard work has gone into developing this site, which is now home for several ponies, donkeys and goats, as well as geese and chickens. There is also open pasture, which has been given over to wildlife and a blacksmith's forge.

Facilities include a café and picnic areas.
BR Barking
❏ 369, 387
Open: daily, 8.30 a.m.– 4.30 p.m.

Vauxhall City Farm

24 St Oswald's Place (entrance in Tyers Street), Lambeth, SE11 (0171 582 4204)
An excellently equipped city farm with plenty of facilities, overlooked, bizarrely, by the new MI6 building in Vauxhall. There are dozens of animals, from pigs, piglets, hens, sheep, ducks and geese to rabbits and hens. Children can also ride on the two ponies and the donkey.

Facilities include a shop, a visitors' centre and a spinning and weaving club.
⊖ Kennington
❏ 77, 322, 344
Open: Tuesday–Thursday, Saturday and Sunday, 10.30 a.m.–5.30 p.m.

ZOOS AND ANIMAL ENCLOSURES

London Butterfly House at Syon Park

Park Road and London Road, Brentford, Middlesex TW8 (0181 560 7272)
Tropical greenhouse gardens and ponds with hundreds of free-flying butterflies from all over the world. Among the most interesting are the painted lady, red admiral, orange tip, holly blue, large white, silver spotted skipper and small tortoiseshell. Displays of insects under glass include locusts, scorpions, spiders, stick insects and leaf-cutter ants.
BR Syon Lane
❏ 116, 117, 237, 267
Open: daily, 10.00 a.m.–5.30 p.m.

London Zoo

Regent's Park, NW1 (0171 722 3333)
See also page 49
London Zoo is one of the oldest and best-known zoological gardens in the world. It was founded in 1829 to increase our knowledge of animal life and, more than 150 years later, it is still making exciting new discoveries about the world around us.

Today, in an age of conflict between the developing world and the survival of our natural world, the zoo's work is more important than ever. Its discoveries are helping to save the natural balance that the animal world brings to the planet. An important element in this work is breeding endangered species and, wherever possible, replenishing natural populations.

There are over 12,000 animals in the zoo and there is always something special to watch or join in with, from pelican feeding to spider encounters, shows and rides. Highlights of the Zoo include the Elephant House – where three Asian elephants live side by side with two rare black rhinos – and the Penguin Pool, a recently restored architectural masterpiece designed by Lubetkin.

Facilities include shops, restaurants and cafés.

FOR THE ZOO
Book to REGENT'S PARK or CAMDEN TOWN
UNDERGROUND

⊖ Camden Town

❏ C2, 274

P meters on the perimeter road (free after 1.30 p.m. Saturday, all day Sunday) or London Zoo's car park (££)

Open: daily, 10.00 a.m.–5.30 p.m. (summer), 10.00 a.m. –5.00 p.m. (winter), including bank holidays; closed Christmas Day

££

Battersea Park Children's Zoo

Battersea, SW11 (0181 871 7530)
See also page 27
A lively zoo with plenty of opportunity for children to get involved with the animals – there is a special 'animal contact' area where you can mix with goats and pigs. The meerkats are always entertaining and there are also stables, a reptile house, various exotic birds, as well as wallabies and emus from Australia.

⊖ Sloane Square
BR Battersea Park
❏ 19, 44, 45A, 49, 137, 137A, 239, 249, 319, 344
Open: May–September, daily, 11.00 a.m.–6.00 p.m. (5.30 p.m. last admission); October–April, weekends only
£

Brent Lodge Park

Church Road, Hanwell, W7 (0181 566 1919)
Children love this park's unusual menagerie. Outside, in an enclosure, donkeys, wallabies and sheep live contentedly side by side, along with rabbits, squirrels and guinea pigs. Inside the zoo are some marmosets and monkeys, a reptile section with lizards and scorpions, and a piranha tank.
BR Hanwell
❏ E1, E3, E4, E8, 83, 207, 607X
Open: daily, park opening times

Corams Fields

93 Guildford Street, WC1 (0171 937 6138)
Right in the heart of Bloomsbury is an unusual park full of farm animals and pets which adults are allowed to visit only if they are accompanied by a child. There is also an aviary, a children's nursery and playground areas.
⊖ Russell Square
❑ 7, 17, 45, 46, 68, 91, 168, 188
Open: March–October, daily, 9.00 a.m.– 6.00 p.m.; November–February, daily, 9.00 a.m.–5.00 p.m.

Clissold Park

Green Lanes, Stoke Newington, N16 (0181 254 9736)
See also page 20
Clissold Park was one of the first municipal parks to have a zoo. In fact, it is really an animal enclosure, housing peacocks, cranes and deer. There is also an aviary with small, colourful, exotic birds.
⊖ Manor House
❑ 73, 106, 141, 171A
Open: daily

Golders Hill Park

Golders Hill, NW11 (0171 485 4491/0181 455 5183)
See also page 21
Colourful flamingos live on a small lake near the flower garden. Elsewhere, in an enclosure, you can see deer, wallabies, goats and exotic birds such as the Sarus crane.
⊖ Golders Green
❑ H2, 13, 28, 83, 102, 183, 210, 226, 240, 245, 268
Open: daily, park opening times

Greenwich Park

Greenwich, SE10 (0181 858 2608)
See also page 52
About thirty fallow and roe deer are kept in an enclosure here and have been a feature of the park since the sixteenth century.
BR Greenwich
❑ 177, 180, 286, 386
Open: daily, park opening times

Holland Park

Kensington, W11 (0171 602 2226)
See also page 13
At the wooded north end of the park is a penned-off enclosure. Entry is not allowed, but from the path outside you can see peacocks, pheasants, rabbits and squirrels.
⊖ High Street Kensington, Holland Park
❑ C1, 9, 9A, 10, 27, 28, 31, 49, 52, 70, 94
Open: daily, park opening times

Horniman Gardens

Forest Hill, SE23 (0181 699 2339)
See also page 30
At one end of these gardens is a small zoo, with a selection of goats, rabbits and turkeys, as well as a number of caged birds.
BR Forest Hill
❑ P4, P13, 63, 122, 171, 176, 185, 312
Open: daily, park opening times

St James's Park

SW1 (0171 839 1793)
See also page 50
St James's Park has long been associated with unusual and exotic birds. Birdcage Walk is so called after the aviaries built by King Charles II. Today the aviaries have gone, but there is an enormous number of birds here still, some tame enough to eat out of your hand. The most famous are the pelicans, who live in a sanctuary by the lake – try to arrive in time to watch them having tea at 3.00 p.m. There are dozens of friendly, and greedy, ducks, geese, sparrows and pigeons here too.
⊖ St James's Park, Westminster
❑ 11, 24, 211, 507
Open: daily, park opening times

Victoria Park

Old Ford Road and Grove Road, South Hackney, E9 (0181 985 1957)
See also page 39
Victoria Park has a small enclosure where deer live happily alongside rabbits and guinea pigs.
⊖ Mile End
BR Cambridge Heath
❑ D6, 26, 48, 55, 106, 253, 277
Open: daily, park opening times

7

GARDENERS' LONDON

NOT ONLY is London well served with parks and green spaces for walks, sports and picnics; there are also dozens of public and botanic gardens waiting to be discovered too. Most people will have heard of the famous Royal Botanic Gardens at Kew, but did you know about Brockwell Park's walled Shakespearian Garden or the Barbican Centre's blossoming conservatory.

If you want to learn more about the history of gardening, an excellent starting point is the Museum of Garden History next to Lambeth Palace. This is a unique museum, set in the recently restored St Mary's church. If you are looking for inspiration for your own London garden, visit any of the public and private gardens listed below. For extra information, the National Gardens Scheme produces a useful annual guide, known as 'The Yellow Book', giving the dates when private London gardens are open to the public. For more information, phone the County Organizer on 01932 864532.

BOTANIC GARDENS

Avery Hill

Avery Hill Road, Eltham, SE9 (0181 850 2666)
The Winter Garden, a large red-brick conservatory, stands bleakly on Avery Hill, facing south across the suburbs. Inside, its musty, damp atmosphere makes you feel time has stood still here since it was first built in the nineteenth century. In fact, this Victorian jungle is alive and well, with fascinating palms, ferns and exotic plants, as well as a small aviary with parrots, other birds and even a squirrel, all of which make it an unusual and interesting place to explore.
BR Eltham Park, Falconwood
❏ B13, 132, 228, 233, 328
Open: Monday–Sunday 10.00 a.m.–4.00 p.m. (closed 1.00 p.m.–2.00 p.m.)

❖

Chelsea Physic Garden

Royal Hospital Road, Chelsea, SW3 (0171 352 5646)

The Chelsea Physic Garden was founded in 1673 by the Apothecaries' Company for the collection, study and dissemination of plants with medicinal value and is one of Europe's oldest botanic gardens. The 1.6 hectares (4 acres) are divided into a number of small areas, from a garden showing the history of medicinal plants to an ethnobotanical Garden of World Medicine (which depicts various plants from around the world and their use in medicine), botanical beds, glasshouses and many rare plants, such as the largest olive tree outdoors in Britain.

In the centre of the grounds stands a statue of Sir Hans Sloane, an eighteenth-century surgeon who became patron of the Chelsea Physic Garden and introduced many plants to this country. Today, the Physic Garden still maintains its traditional roles of research and education, as well as serving the interests of visitors. A historical walk is being laid out to tell the Garden's own history and that of plant introduction and plant naming. The English Gardening School, based here, also offers a wide range of adult education courses on garden design.

After looking round the garden, there are plenty of secluded corners where you can rest, and with tea and homemade cakes available as well, you feel you are in an old friend's country garden rather than central London.

⊖ Sloane Square

❏ C1, 11, 19, 22, 137, 137A, 211, 239, 319

Open: April–October, Wednesday–Saturday, 2.00 p.m.–5.00 p.m.

£

Fulham Palace Grounds and Botanic Gardens

Fulham Palace Road, Fulham, SW6 (0171 736 7181)

See also page 42

Fulham Palace was originally the summer retreat of the Bishop of London. As early as the sixteenth century the palace gardens were famous for growing rare and exotic plants and trees. Bishop Grundal (1559–70) sent grapes grown here to Queen Elizabeth I and planted the evergreen oak in the corner of the gardens. Near this tree is the walled kitchen garden with a knot garden, botanic beds and wistaria walk. In the late seventeenth and early eighteenth centuries, Bishop Compton (1675–1713) imported many rare species from overseas, including the magnolia which he grew for the first time in Europe at Fulham. Many of his trees and shrubs are still represented in these gardens.

⊖ Putney Bridge

❏ C4, 14, 74, 220

Open: daily, 9.00 a.m.–dusk

Hampton Court Palace Gardens

Hampton Court Road, Hampton, Surrey KT8 (0181 977 8441)

See also page 51

Hampton Court is famed not only for its splendid architecture and colourful past residents, but also for its gardens. Some 500 years of royal gardening history are spread across 24 hectares (60 acres) and all the monarchs who lived at Hampton Court have left their individual mark here.

❖

As much a display of royal power as a source of pleasure, the gardens were originally dominated by heraldic beasts on painted and gilded poles, reminding courtiers and foreign visitors alike of the might of the Tudor dynasty. Subsequent developments saw the gardens change completely from the pomp and grandeur of William and Mary's formal Dutch garden to the natural landscaping of the Georgian era. By the time Queen Victoria opened the site to the public, the gardens were very much the fascinating blend of styles seen today.

Royal gardeners have always been fond of the new and exotic and Hampton Court has been home to many botanical treasures, including newly discovered species from Africa and America. However, the most famous plant in the garden is the Great Vine, planted by Capability Brown in 1769, while other major attractions include the Maze, which was created in the early eighteenth century.

As well as being home for Henry VIII's famous real tennis courts, arbours and covered walkways, such as the laburnum walk at the wilderness end, the garden was perfect for leisurely walks for courtiers and now for visitors. It was functional too; the ornamental pools of Henry VIII's pond garden were originally stocked with freshwater fish for the kitchens and many of the flowerbeds were planted with culinary and medicinal herbs, while the orangery provided exotic fruits.

Today Hampton Court is the venue for an annual flower show held in July (see page 194).

BR Hampton Wick

❏ R68, 111, 411, 726X

〰 boat from Westminster, Charing Cross, Richmond, Kingston

P Bushy Park (free) or Hampton Court car park (££)

£ (for entry to house)

Open: mid–March–mid–October, 9.30 a.m.– 6.00 p.m., except Mondays, 10.15 a.m. – 6.00 p.m.; mid–October–mid–March, 9.30 a.m.– 4.30 p.m., except Mondays, 10.15 a.m. – 4.30 p.m.

Museum of Garden History

St Mary-at-Lambeth, Lambeth Road, Lambeth, SE1 (0171 633 9701)
This museum provides a fascinating insight into the history of gardening through a permanent exhibition and regular lectures.

Outside is the Tradescant Garden, which contains only plants grown by the Tradescant family and other plants from the seventeenth century. The two Tradescants, father and son, were gardeners, successively, to the 1st Lord Salisbury, the Duke of Buckingham and then King Charles I and Henrietta Maria, and brought back from their travels in Europe and America many of the flowers, shrubs and trees we take for granted today.

They planted these exotic species, such as the African marigold, the tulip tree, the Virginia creeper, bergamot and columbine, in their famous garden in Lambeth, which became well known as the most extensive plant collection in England in the seventeenth century. They also collected 'all things strange and true' and displayed these in their house in Lambeth, which, together with the garden, became a popular place for the Royal Court and the nobility of the day to visit. This collection ultimately formed the basis of the Ashmolean Museum in Oxford, where much of it can still be seen in the Founders' Room.

The Tradescants are buried in the churchyard at St Mary-at-Lambeth, next to the tomb of Admiral Bligh of the HMS *Bounty*. The church was closed in 1972 in a sad state of dereliction, but a public appeal to save it was launched in 1977 and the work of restoration has continued steadily.

⊖ Lambeth North, Waterloo, Westminster
BR Waterloo
❏ 3, C10, 12, 53, 109, 159, 344
Open: Monday–Friday, 11.00 a.m.–3.00 p.m.; Sunday, 10.30 a.m.–5.00 p.m.
Donations welcome

Queen Mary's Garden and Nesfield Gardens

Regent's Park, NW1 (0171 486 7095)
See also page 49
In 1830 a botanic garden was developed in the centre of the park and this in turn gave way to Queen Mary's Garden. Today, it houses an extensive collection of both modern and old roses. The garden also contains impressive herbaceous borders, a begonia garden, a fuchsia border, alpine plants and water features. In the outer park are the famous Nesfield Gardens, a massive display of bedding plants which are changed seasonally to make use of a wide range of plants, many of which are rarely seen on display in public parks.

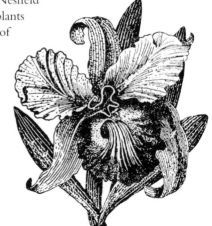

⊖ Baker Street, Camden Town, Chalk Farm, Great Portland Street, Regent's Park
BR Primrose Hill
❏ 2, C2, 13, 18, 27, 30, 74, 82, 113, 135, 139, 159, 274
P two car parks in Regent's Park, one near the zoo, the other near Gloucester Gate. Parking is also permitted along the Outer Circle after 11.00 a.m.
Open: daily, 5.00 a.m. (or dawn)– dusk

❖

Royal Botanic Gardens

Kew Road, Richmond, Surrey TW9 (0181 332 5607)

Kew is undoubtedly the prize botanic garden in London, with 120 hectares (300 acres) of landscaped gardens and over 50,000 different plants from all over the world. There is so much to see there that you can go back endlessly without ever becoming bored – where else is it possible to stroll through a rain forest, wander across a desert and visit a South American swamp all on a cold winter's day in London?

Kew has a number of massive greenhouses, including the Temperate House, which shelters hundreds of Mediterranean and South African species, the recently renovated Waterlily House (closed in winter) and the state-of-the-art Princess of Wales Conservatory, with ten different climatic zones.

The displays in the glasshouses create a wonderful atmosphere. The most spectacular of them all is the famous Palm House, which provides a grand Victorian centrepiece to the gardens. Designed by the architect Decimus Burton and the engineer Richard Turner, it is constructed entirely from iron and glass and took four years to build (1844–8). Inside are dozens of tropical plants from Asia, South America and Africa, such as coffee, cocoa and tea.

Other interesting buildings at Kew include the 50-metre (163-foot) Great Pagoda, the Marianne North Gallery, Queen Charlotte's Cottage and Kew Palace (separate charge). There is also a large collection of trees, shrubs, herbaceous and alpine plants.

⊖ Kew Gardens

BR Kew Bridge, Kew Gardens

❏ R61, 65, R68, 391

Open: galleries daily, 9.30 a.m.–4.30 p.m.; Sunday, 9.30 a.m.–5.30 p.m.; *glasshouses* daily, 10.00 a.m.–4.30 p.m.; Sunday, 10.00 a.m.–5.30 p.m. or earlier in winter; *park* daily, 10.00 a.m.–dusk (latest 8 p.m.)

£

Kew Gardens

Kew Gardens' official name is the Royal Botanic Gardens, and they date back to when George III's mother, Augusta, started a botanical garden on the site in 1759. Open to the public since 1841, the gardens have become a major institute for botanical research. Among the garden's achievements are the introduction of breadfruit to the West Indies in 1791 (the purpose of Captain Bligh's voyage on the *Bounty*), quinine to India in 1860 and rubber trees to Malaysia in 1875. In the late nineteenth century Kew played an important part in restoring the European wine industry after it was wiped out by disease. Today, in response to the developing environmental crisis, scientists from Kew Gardens are cataloguing the incredible diversity of the tropical regions (areas like the rain forest contain a staggering 90,000 of the world's 250,000 known flowering plants).

KEW GARDENS

South Lambeth Botanical Institute
323 Norwood Road, Herne Hill, SE24 (0181 674 5787)
A small botanic garden, formally laid out with many rare and interesting species of plants.
BR Herne Hill, Tulse Hill
❏ 2, 3, 37, 68, 68A, 115, 196, 322
Open: Monday, 9.00 a.m.–4.00 p.m. (all other times by appointment only)
Donations welcome

Syon Park
Park Road and London Road, Brentford, Middlesex TW8 (0181 560 0881)
Syon House and Park, which belong to the Duke of Northumberland, are wonderfully situated on a curve of the Thames opposite Kew Gardens. The gardens, which extend to the river, were beautifully designed by Capability Brown between 1767 and 1773.

There is an enormous rose garden, the Butterfly House (see page 105) and the Great Conservatory, designed by Charles Fowler in 1820–27. Inside the conservatory are cacti, small free-flying birds and an aquarium.
BR Brentford Central, Syon Lane
❏ 116, 117, 237, 267
Open: house Good Friday–end September, 12 a.m.–4.15 p.m. (closed Friday and Saturday); *park* summer, 10.00 a.m.–6 p.m.; winter, 1.00 p.m.–dusk
£ (for entry to house)

PUBLIC GARDENS

Alexander Pope's Grotto
St. Catherine's School, Cross Deep, Twickenham, Middlesex TW1 (0181 892 1201)
The famous grotto of Alexander Pope, the Augustan poet, still survives, consisting of a hand-dug tunnel decorated with rocks, shells and glass.
BR Twickenham
❏ 33, R68
Open: Saturday afternoon by appointment with the school principal only; phone for more information

Barbican Conservatory
Silk Street, EC2 (0171 638 4141)
The City of London's largest conservatory and part of the Barbican Centre. An extensive collection of temperate plants includes palms, orchids and climbers and there is a good variety of cacti and succulents.
⊖ Barbican, Moorgate
❏ 4, 21, 43, X43, 56, 76, 133, 141, 172, 214, 271
Open: Saturday 12 a.m.–4.00 p.m.; Sunday, 12 a.m.–5.30 p.m.
£

Brockwell Park

Dulwich Road and Norwood Road, Herne Hill, SE24 (0181 674 6141)
See also page 28
When the Brockwell estate became a public park in 1892, the walled kitchen was turned into a Shakespearian Garden, a magnificent 'secret' garden in the centre of otherwise plain grounds. The elegant house has unfortunately fallen into a state of disrepair and is now almost hidden from view by sheets of vandalized metal.
⊖ Brixton
BR Herne Hill
❑ 3, 37, 68, 68A, 196, 322
Open: daily

Cannizaro Park

West Side, Wimbledon, SW19 (0181 879 1464)
This delightful park features a water garden, a formal rose garden, a kitchen garden and an azalea dell. It also has wooded walks and sloping lawns which are overlooked by the elegant Cannizaro House. Once the home of landed gentry and later an officers' convalescent home, it has been beautifully refurbished and is now a hotel where you can sit and have tea on the terrace.
⊖/**BR** Wimbledon
❑ 93, 200
Open: daily, dawn–dusk

Chiswick House

Burlington Lane, Chiswick, W4 (0181 994 3299)
The grounds of Chiswick House are, historically, among the most important in England, for it was here that Lord Burlington (1695–1753) and William Kent (1684–1748) experimented with the natural style of gardening.

Interesting features of this garden include the Ionic Temple, the Orange Tree Garden and the beautiful Italian Garden, designed in the eighteenth century by Lewis Kennedy from Hammersmith. Kennedy had previously worked for the Empress Josephine in Paris and introduced roses to England from France.
⊖ Gunnersbury
❑ E3, 190, 290
Open: daily

College Gardens

Westminster Abbey, SW1 (0171 222 5152)
Good collection of old English herbs within fourteenth-century river walls.
⊖ Westminster
❑ 11, 24, 88, 211
Open: Thursday, 10.00 a.m.–6.00 p.m.

Fenton House

Windmill Hill, Hampstead, NW3 (0171 435 3471)
Fenton House, one of the best William and Mary houses surviving intact in London, has an excellent collection of early keyboard instruments inside, while

outside is one of the most attractive gardens in London. It is set on three levels and has recently been beautifully restored to its original design.

⊖ Hampstead

❑ 46, 210, 268

Open: October–March, Saturday and Sunday, 2.00 a.m.–6.00 p.m.; April–October, Saturday, Sunday and bank holidays, 11.00 a.m.–6.00 p.m.; Monday–Wednesday, 1.00 a.m.–7.00 p.m.

£ (for entry to National Trust house)

Geffrye Museum

Kingsland Road, Shoreditch, E2 (0171 739 9893)

The Geffrye Museum is a fascinating collection of almshouses and a chapel depicting the evolution of furniture and household appliances through a series of small rooms arranged in chronological order from 1600 to the present day. Outside, in a courtyard, there are plane trees planted in 1712–19 by the Ironmongers' Company with a bequest left by Sir Robert Geffrye, Lord Mayor of London, and, behind the almshouses, an attractive herb garden.

Derelict until 1990, the herb garden was reopened in 1992. It comprises over 200 herbs, including those grown in the London garden of the seventeenth-century herbalist John Gerard, as well as roses and honeysuckle, and is designed on a traditional plan of beds intersected by geometric paths.

⊖ Old Street

❑ 22A, 22B, 67, 149, 243, 243A

Open: Tuesday–Saturday, 10.00 a.m.–5.00 p.m.; Sunday, 2.00 p.m.–5.00 p.m.; closed Monday (garden only open April–October)

Ham House

Ham, Surrey TW10 (0181 940 1950)

The spectacular gardens to the east and south of house have been restored to their seventeenth-century appearance by the National Trust.

⊖/**BR** Richmond

❑ 65, 371

Open: gardens daily; *house* Tuesday–Sunday, 11.a.m.–5.00 p.m.

£ (for entry to National Trust house)

Horniman Gardens

100 London Road, Forest Hill, SE23 (0181 699 2339)

See also page 30, page 155

Within the park's 6 hectares (16 acres) there is much to delight gardeners, such as a water garden, rose garden and formal sunken garden, as well as regular gardening demonstrations.

The gardens were part of Frederick Horniman's home in Forest Hill and the magnificent conservatory once stood at the Horniman's family home at Coombe Cliff in Croydon. It was reconstructed here by English Heritage in 1989.

BR Forest Hill

❑ P4, P13, 63, 122, 171, 176, 185, 312

Open: daily, 8.00 a.m.–dusk

KENWOOD

UNDERGROUND
to GOLDERS GREEN
or HIGHGATE STATION
thence by bus 210
to "The Spaniards"
Daily every 7½ minutes

TRAM
3, 5 to HAMPSTEAD
7, 15 to HIGHGATE Rd.
11 to HIGHGATE VILLAGE
from Moorgate or Holborn
Daily every 5 minutes

Kenwood House Gardens

Hampstead Lane, NW3 (0181 348 1286)

Although adjoining Hampstead Heath, Kenwood has its own, quite separate atmosphere. A beautiful eighteenth-century house, now owned by English Heritage, its gardens are a mix of formal and informal. If you walk down the sloping grass lawns to the lake at the bottom, you can then go on either across the heath towards Highgate or to Hampstead.

Nearer the house, the gardens are more formal, with a covered walkway and attractive flowerbeds. The lake is also the location for regular summer outdoor concerts.

⊖ Golders Green,
BR Hampstead Heath
❑ 210

Open: April–September daily, 10.00 a.m.–6.00 p.m.; October–March, daily, 10.00 a.m.–4.00 p.m.

The lake, Kenwood House Gardens

❖

Lambeth Palace

Lambeth Palace Road, Lambeth, SE1 (0171 928 8282)
The second largest private (occasionally opened to public) garden in London after the Queen's at Buckingham Palace, this land has been in the hands of the Archbishop of Canterbury since the end of the twelfth century. A significant renewal of the garden has taken place over the past few years under the direction of Rosalind Runcie, wife of the former archbishop. Interesting features include a restored rose walk, a new border, a herb garden, a wild garden, rhododendrons, spring bulbs and camelias.
⊖ Lambeth, Westminster
❑ D1, 3, C10, D11, P11, 12, 53, 76, 77, 109, 159, 171A, 211, 344, 507
Open: as part of the National Gardens Scheme only; see 'The Yellow Book'
£ (for charity)

Marble Hill House and Park

Richmond Road, Twickenham, Middlesex TW1 (0181 892 5715)
See also page 71
This beautiful Palladian house was built in the 1720s for George II's mistress, Henrietta Howard, the Countess of Suffolk, and was later occupied by Mrs Fitzherbert, the mistress of King George IV. Looking out across the river towards Petersham meadows, the park was originally laid out between 1723 and 1729. Today it is regularly used for summertime evening concerts (see page 155) and it is also of interest to gardeners. There is a splendid selection of trees, including horse chestnuts, Lombardy poplars and an eighteenth-century black walnut. The

Marble Hill House

original ice-house, where ice was stored during the winter, is worth visiting too.
BR St Margaret's, Twickenham
❑ H22, 33, R68, R70, 90, 290
Open: daily

Museum of London: Garden Court

London Wall, EC2 (0171 600 0807)
This garden offers a fascinating guide through the history of plantsmanship in London.
⊖ Moorgate
❑ 4, 21, 43, X43, 56, 76, 133, 141, 172, 214, 271
Open: daily, except Mondays

Osterley Park

Jersey Road, Osterley, Isleworth, Middlesex TW7 (0181 560 3918)
The first house at Osterley was built in Tudor times and had an enclosed formal
garden, similar to those at Hampton Court Palace. Both were totally transformed
in the eighteenth century. The house was decorated and furnished for the banker
Robert Child by William Chambers and Robert Adam, while the gardens were
replaced with a large, landscape park complete with lakes and an avenue of trees
leading to the house. The greenhouse was designed by Robert Adam, while the
Doric Temple and birdcage were created by William Chambers.
⊖ Osterley
BR Thornbury Road
❑ H91, 110, 111, 120
Open: daily, 10.00 a.m.–8.00 p.m. (or dusk)

Roof Gardens

99 Kensington High Street, W8 (0171 937 7994)
This wonderful roof garden was once the centrepiece of Derry and Tom's
department store, which later became the Biba boutique in the 1960s. When the
shop closed down, the gardens became a private club, but non-members are still
allowed to visit them if they make an appointment. It is worth going as these are
some of the most unusual gardens in London. Arranged into Spanish, Tudor and
Japanese settings, the 0.6-hectare (1½ -acre) garden includes tulips, magnolias,
oaks and elms.

The largest tree on the roof is a 9.5-metre (31-foot) poplar and the oldest is a
yew transplanted from a country garden. There is also a woodland glade and a
small pool.
⊖ High Street Kensington
❑ 9A, 28, 31
Open: Monday–Saturday, 9.00 a.m.–5.00 p.m.

Royal Hospital Grounds

Chelsea Embankment, Chelsea, SW3
Many people associate the Royal Hospital grounds with the Chelsea Flower
Show, which is held here every May (see page 190), but they certainly should
not be ignored for the rest of the year. The gardens lie next to the Royal

Hospital, home of the Chelsea Pensioners, and so have always been closely linked with the armed forces. South from the entrance on Royal Hospital Road are Ranelagh Gardens, developed over the former house and gardens of Lord Ranelagh, Paymaster General to the Forces in 1690, a secluded leafy area and a quiet place to sit and read.

The rest of the grounds give excellent views of the Royal Hospital. Originally, the gardens extended to the river, but today they are cut short by a busy road, the Chelsea Embankment.

⊖ Sloane Square

❑ C1, 11, 19, 22, 137, 137A, 211, 239, 249

Open: Monday–Saturday, 10.00a.m.–12.00noon, 2.00p.m.–4.00p.m.

Overleaf: Epsom

❖

SPORTING
LONDON

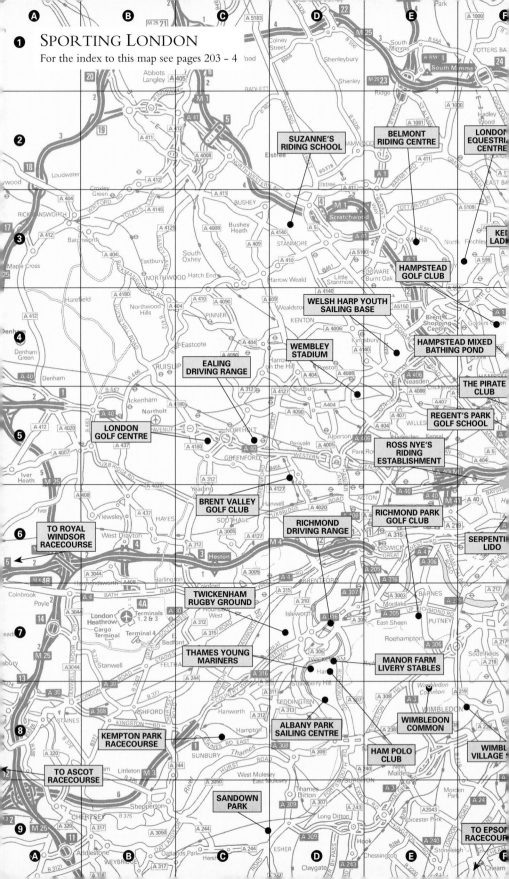

SPORTING LONDON

For the index to this map see pages 203 – 4

SUZANNE'S RIDING SCHOOL

BELMONT RIDING CENTRE

LONDON EQUESTRIAN CENTRE

HAMPSTEAD GOLF CLUB

WELSH HARP YOUTH SAILING BASE

HAMPSTEAD MIXED BATHING POND

WEMBLEY STADIUM

THE PIRATE CLUB

EALING DRIVING RANGE

REGENT'S PARK GOLF SCHOOL

LONDON GOLF CENTRE

ROSS NYE'S RIDING ESTABLISHMENT

BRENT VALLEY GOLF CLUB

RICHMOND DRIVING RANGE

RICHMOND PARK GOLF CLUB

SERPENTINE LIDO

TO ROYAL WINDSOR RACECOURSE

TWICKENHAM RUGBY GROUND

THAMES YOUNG MARINERS

MANOR FARM LIVERY STABLES

KEMPTON PARK RACECOURSE

ALBANY PARK SAILING CENTRE

WIMBLEDON COMMON

WIMBLEDON VILLAGE

TO ASCOT RACECOURSE

HAM POLO CLUB

SANDOWN PARK

TO EPSOM RACECOURSE

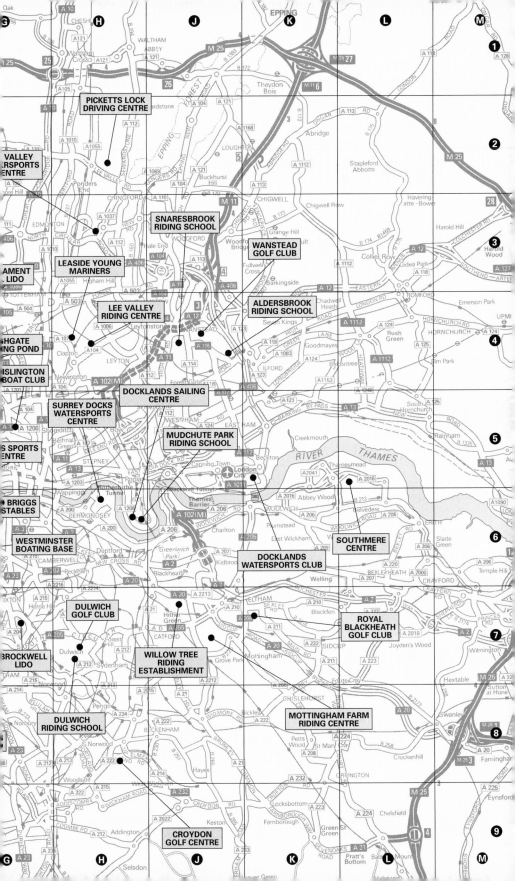

8
OUTDOOR SPORTS

I F YOU enjoy sport and live in London, there is no need to feel restricted to the odd game of squash or the occasional aerobics class. London has a wealth of outdoor sporting facilities to suit all interests and standards, from jet skiing in Docklands to orienteering on Barnes Common and playing netball in Lincoln's Inn.

In addition, London has some of the most famous sports venues in the world, such as Wimbledon, Wembley Stadium and Lord's Cricket Ground. Full details of where to go to watch your favourite sport are given in each entry.

HOW TO FIND A SPORT

Below is a brief guide to the sports available for both the able-bodied and the disabled. They have been listed in alphabetical order, with information on where to play, where to spectate (if applicable), opening times of venues and how to get there (if applicable) and the associated recognized bodies.

ANGLING

London offers plenty of good places to fish, from the Thames and the canals to small lakes and reservoirs. Before casting your line, though, make sure you have the necessary permits, as fishing rights in most sites are owned by individuals, fishing clubs or the London Anglers' Association. To find out where to fish and to buy the necessary rod licence, contact the National Rivers Authority.

The recognized body is:
London Anglers' Association, Forest Road Hall, Hervey Park Road, E17 6LJ (0181 520 7477)

ARCHERY

For details on London's archery ranges contact the:
Grand National Archery Society (GNAS), National Agricultural Centre, 7th Street, Stoneleigh, Kenilworth, Warwickshire CV8 2LG (01203 696631)

ATHLETICS

If you want to take athletics seriously you will need to join a local club so you can take part in competitive events and have the chance of using equipment such as hurdles and javelins, which are only ever available to club members.

For spectating, Crystal Palace National Sports Centre, Anerley Road, SE19 (box office: 0181 778 0131), is the major athletics venue in Britain. For details of

Fishing on the Thames at Greenwich

forthcoming events either phone or pop along (**BR** Crystal Palace) on any weekday between 9.30 a.m. and 5.00 p.m. For more information about the annual London Marathon, see page 189.

The recognized body is:

Southern Counties Athletics Association, 19 Malborough Lane, Charlton, SE7 7DE (0181 856 9482)

BOWLS

In addition to a handful of privately owned bowling greens, there are several public ones in London's parks, including:

Battersea Park, SW11 (0181 871 7530)
Brockwell Park, SE24 (0181 674 6141)
Clissold Park, N16 (0171 254 9736)
Dulwich Park, SE21 (0181 693 5737)

The recognized body is:

English Bowling Association, Lyndhurst Road, Worthing, West Sussex BN11 2AZ (01903 820222)

CANOEING

(See pages 142–5)

CRICKET

Contact the London Community Cricket Association (0171 708 1686) to find your local club. Most parks have cricket nets or pitches available for casual games.

To spectate, Lord's, St John's Wood Road, NW8 (Underground: St John's Wood; box office: 0171 289 8979) and the Oval, Kennington, SE11 (Underground: Oval; box office: 0171 582 6660) are the two county cricket grounds in London.

The recognized body is:

National Cricket Association (NCA), Lord's Cricket Ground, St John's Wood Road, NW8 8QZ (0171 289 6098)

CROQUET

If your garden is large enough, croquet is fun to play at home. If you want to take it more seriously, you will need to join a private club, the most prestigious of which is the Hurlingham Club, as there are no public croquet grounds in London.

The recognized body is:

The Croquet Association, c/o The Hurlingham Club, Ranelagh Gardens, SW6 3PR (0171 736 3148)

CYCLING

The past decade has seen an explosion in the popularity of cycling in London, thanks in part to the success of the mountain bike – great fun and ideal for

---

Cycling in London

For your safety, make sure you're clearly visible by wearing a reflective belt or arm band. You can also buy self-adhesive reflective material – the best is Reflexite – cutting it into strips and sticking it on your bike.

At night make sure you have a good set of front and back lights. Dusk is probably the most dangerous time for accidents, so turn your lights on as soon as the light begins to fade.

We all know that the traffic in London is appalling, but at least cyclists can be assured that they are exercising *and* getting to their destination. However, cyclists need to keep on their toes all the time, even when the traffic is slow-moving, as drivers sometimes do the unexpected, such as suddenly turning left without indicating or opening a car door without looking behind them. The best advice is to keep to the left of the carriageway about 1 metre (3 feet) away from the curb, where you will be visible to cars overtaking or approaching from side roads.

coping with the lumps and bumps in the roads – and also to the pioneering work of the London Cycling Campaign, which strives to improve conditions and provisions for all cyclists in London.

As well as campaigning on issues such as cycle routes and improving the roads for cyclists, the London Cycling Campaign (LCC) runs maintenance classes, a 'Bikemate' scheme for novices, gives free legal advice, has regular social rides and has arranged discounts at many bike shops in London.

The LCC also produce a useful handbook, *On Your Bike*, which is essential reading for all cyclists. It covers maintenance, safety and has a useful map showing all the cycle routes in London. They can be contacted at 3 Stamford Street, SE1 (0171 928 7220).

FOOTBALL

Football can be played almost anywhere in London – most parks provide pitches and some even have all-weather surfaces too for casual games. If you would like to join an amateur team, contact the London Division of the Football Association, Aldworth Grove, Lewisham, SE13 6HY (0181 690 9626).

London is home to many of Britain's best football teams, all playing matches regularly in the season (approximately August to May). For details of forthcoming matches, keep an eye on the sports pages of newspapers and specialist football magazines.

The recognized body is:
The Football Association, 16 Lancaster Gate, W2 3LW (0171 262 4542)

GOLF

For those wanting to learn:

Regent's Park Golf (and Tennis) School
Outer Circle, Regent's Park, NW1 (0171 724 0634)
Teaches beginners through to advance players on putting greens and bunkers and has a 'made to measure' club service.
⊖ Regent's Park
❑ C2, 18, 27, 30, 274
Open: daily, 8.00 a.m.–9.00 p.m.
££

Brent Valley Golf Club

Church Road, Hanwell, W7 (0181 567 1287)
Type of course: public meadowland
Length: 18 holes, 5,021 metres (5,440 yards)
Visitors: welcome on weekdays and at weekends
££

Dulwich and Sydenham Hill

Grange Lane, College Road, SE21 (0181 693 3961)
Type of course: parkland
Length: 18 holes, 5,585 metres (6,051 yards)
Visitors: welcome at weekends, with prior arrangement
££

Hampstead Golf Club

Winnington Road, Hampstead, N2 (0181 455 0203)
Type of course: parkland
Length: 9 holes, 5,364 metres (5,812 yards)
Visitors: welcome on weekdays (not Tuesdays), but book first; time is restricted at weekends
££

Richmond Park Golf Club

Richmond Park, SW15 (0181 876 3205)
Type of course: parkland
Length: 18 holes, 5,506 metres (5,965 yards)
Visitors: welcome on weekdays, but book first
££

Royal Blackheath

Court Road, Eltham, SE9 (0181 850 1795)
Type of course: parkland
Length: 18 holes, 5,731 metres (6,209 yards)
Visitors: welcome (bring handicap certificate)
££

Wanstead Golf Club

Overton Drive, Wanstead, E11 (0181 989 3938)
Type of course: parkland
Length: 18 holes, 5,639 (6,109 yards)
Visitors: welcome on weekdays with prior arrangement.
££

❖

Wimbledon Common

Camp Road, Wimbledon, SW19 (0181 946 7571)
Type of course: moorland
Length: 18 holes, 5,019 metres (5,438 yards)
Visitors: welcome on weekdays
££

DRIVING RANGES

Croydon Golf Centre

175 Long Lane, Addiscombe, Surrey CR0 (0181 656 1690)
Twenty-four covered, floodlit bays
Open: Monday–Friday, 10.00 a.m.–10.00 p.m.; Saturday and Sunday, 10.00 a.m.–9.00 p.m.
££

Ealing Driving Range

Rowdell Road, Northolt, Middlesex UB5 (0181 845 4967)
Thirty-six covered, floodlit bays; four open bays
Open: 10.00 a.m.–10.30 p.m.
££

London Golf Centre

Ruislip Road, Northolt, Middlesex UB5 (0181 842 0442)
Twenty covered, floodlit bays
Open: Dawn–10.15 p.m.
££

Picketts Lock Driving Range

Picketts Lock Lane, Edmonton, N9 (0181 803 3611)
Twenty covered, floodlit bays
Open: Monday–Friday, 10.00 a.m.–9.00 p.m.; Saturday and Sunday, 9.00 a.m.–8.00 p.m.
££

Richmond Driving Range

Richmond Athletic Ground, Twickenham, Surrey TW9 (0181 332 5570)
Twenty covered, floodlit bays
Open: 9.30 a.m.–9.30 p.m.
££

HOCKEY

Club matches are played throughout London most weekends. Contact the Southern Counties Hockey Association to find your local team.

The recognized bodies are:

The All-England Women's Hockey Association, 52 High Street, Shrewsbury SY1 1ST (01743 233572)

The Hockey Association, Norfolk House, 102 Saxon Gate West, Milton Keynes, Buckinghamshire MK9 2EP (01908 241100)

HORSERACING

There are a number of racecourses within easy distance of London. The most convenient way to travel there is by car, although it is worth remembering that there will be traffic jams around the racecourse. If you go by train special transport is often laid on during race meets between the station and the racecourse.

Ascot

Ascot, Berkshire SL5 (01344 22211)
Owned by Her Majesty The Queen, Ascot is thought by many to be the premier racecourse in the world. It is best known for Royal Ascot, the race meeting held annually in June over four days. Other major races include the King George VI and the Queen Elizabeth Diamond Stakes, usually held in July. In September is the Ascot Festival, usually held on the third Saturday of the month. The main race is the Queen Elizabeth II stakes – the winner earns the highest prize money in British racing.
BR Ascot
££

Epsom

Epsom, Surrey KT18 (01372 726311)
This is a flat racecourse, so its races are all held in the summer. The main event is the Derby in June, where the winner's owner receives £500,000 prize money.
BR Epsom
££

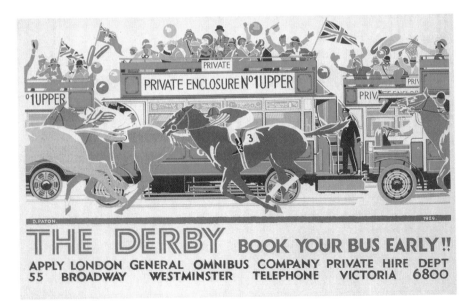

❖

Kempton Park

Sunbury-on-Thames, Middlesex TW16 (01932 782292)
The main meeting at Kempton is over the Christmas period. There are six races on Boxing Day and six more on 27 December. Races are also held throughout the year
BR Kempton Park
❑ 290
££

Royal Windsor

Maidenhead Road, Windsor, Berkshire SL4 (01753 865234)
Royal Windsor has more evening races in the summer than any other racecourse in the country.
BR Windsor
££

Sandown Park

Esher, Surrey KT10 (01372 463072)
Highlights include the Whitbread Gold Cup at the end of April and the Coral Eclipse Stakes in early July. There are also races all year round, including evening ones during the summer.
BR Esher
❑ K3, 218, 415, 427, 501, 511, 513, 527
££

ICE–SKATING

The only outdoor rink in London is at the Broadgate Arena, Eldon Street, EC2.
Open: daily, mid-November–mid-April
    The recognized body is:
The National Skating Association of Great Britain, 15–27 Gee Street, EC1V 3RE (0171 253 3824)

KITE-FLYING

Parliament Hill is one of the most popular spots for kite-flying, but any large open space is suitable. Contact the Kite Store at 69 Neal Street, WC2 (0171 836 1666) for information on local kite-flying competitions and meetings. The recognized body is:

The Kite Society of Great Britain, 31 Grange Road, Ilford, Essex IG1 1EU (0171 836 1666)

LAWN TENNIS

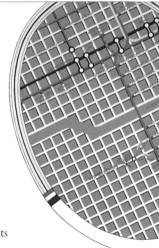

There are over 2,000 public courts in London which are reasonably cheap to hire by the hour. If you want to take the sport more seriously, you have three choices: join a local private tennis club, contact your local borough for information on council-run courses and tournaments or join the Lawn Tennis Association. The latter gives you a national rating, eligibility to play in the singles matches at Lawn Tennis Association official tournaments and, best of all, automatic entry to the Wimbledon ticket ballot. They also have a complete list of clubs and public courts.

The Wimbledon Lawn Tennis Championships and the Stella Artois Championships are the main tennis events in London. See page 193 for more details.

The recognized body is:

The Lawn Tennis Association Trust, London Development Officer, Queen's Club, Palliser Road, W14 9EQ (0171 385 3421)

MOTOR CYCLING

To find out where forthcoming events are taking place in and around London, contact the British Motorcyclists' Federation (see below).

The recognized body is:

The British Motorcyclists' Federation, Central Secretary, Jack Wiley House, 129 Seaforth Avenue, New Malden, Surrey KT3 6JU (0181 942 7914)

MOTOR SPORTS

If you are interested in any type of motor sport, from rallies to Grand Prix, the best way to find out what is going on in and around London is to contact the following recognized body:

London Counties Association of Motor Clubs, 34 Huntingdon Road, Brampton, Huntingdon, Cambridgeshire PE18 8PA (01480 457290)

NETBALL

No longer just a schoolgirls' game, netball has a loyal following with women across London. There are numerous local clubs (contact the All England Netball Association for details of your nearest). If you simply want a casual game, wander along to Lincoln's Inn Fields, WC1, on any evening during the summer.

The recognized body is:

All England Netball Association, Netball House, 9 Paynes Park, Hitchin, Hertfordshire SG5 1EH (01462 442344)

ORIENTEERING

Permanent courses in the London area include:

Abbey Wood, Lesnes Abbey Woods and Bostall Heath, SE2 (0181 310 7494)
Barnes Common, SW13 (0181 878 2359)
Crystal Palace Park, SE24 (0181 778 0612)
Hampstead Heath, NW3 (0171 485 4491)
Lee Valley Park, E4 (01992 713838)

The recognized body is:

British Orienteering Federation (BOF), Riversdale, Dale Road North, Darley Dale, Matlock, Derbyshire DE4 2HX (01629 734042)

For up-to-date information about permanent orienteering courses in the Greater London area, contact The Silva Service, Unit 10, Sky Business Park, Eversley Way, Egham, Surrey TW20 8RF (01784 439193).

PARACHUTING

Obviously it would be impossible to parachute in central London, but there are opportunities to do so close by. Contact the regional office – Miss J. Buckle, c/o Headcorn Parachute Club, Headcorn Airfield, Headcorn, Kent TN27 9HX (01622 890862) – of the recognized body, the British Parachute Association, for more details.

The recognized body is:

British Parachute Association, 5 Wharf Way, Glen Parva, Leicester LE2 9TF (01533 785271)

PARAGLIDING AND HANG–GLIDING

As with parachuting, these sports cannot take place in London. For the nearest local groups, contact the British Hang-gliding and Paragliding Association.

The recognized body is:

The British Hang-gliding and Paragliding Association, The Old School Room, Loughborough Road, Leicester LE4 5JP (01533 611322)

POLO

Contact the Polo Manager at The Equestrian Club, Ham Polo Ground, Richmond, Surrey TW10 (0181 940 2020) for details of where to play.

You can spectate at Guard's Polo Club, Windsor Great Park, Englefield Green, Egham Surrey TW20 OHP (01784 434212). Matches are played every afternoon between May and September and you might even catch a glimpse of Britain's most famous player – HRH The Prince of Wales!

BR Windsor

££

Guard's Polo Club

For those wanting to play or spectate

Ham Polo Ground

Richmond Road, Petersham, Surrey TW10 (0181 398 3263: Secretary)
Matches are played every Sunday afternoon.
BR/⊖ Richmond
❑ H22, 33, H37, R61, 65, R68, R69, R70, 190, 290, 337, 371, 391, 415, 427
££

RIDING

There are seventeen British Horse Society-approved riding schools in London – a surprisingly high count – some of which are listed on pages 137–8.

Aldersbrook Riding School

Empress Avenue, Manor Park, E12 (0181 530 4648)

The school currently has twelve horses, a livery yard and two outdoor maneges. They organize hacks and offer lessons (including lessons for disabled people).

⊖ East Ham, Manor Park, Woodgrange Park

❑ 101

££

Belmont Riding Centre

The Ridgeway, Mill Hill, NW7 (0181 906 1255)

This riding centre offers private and class lessons, as well as hacks. Facilities include a livery yard, two outdoor maneges and an indoor arena.

BR Mill Hill

❑ 113, 114, 186, 221, 240, 251, 302

££

Dulwich Riding School

Dulwich Common, SE21 (0181 693 2944)

There are thirteen horses here and the school provides lessons for children over ten years of age and adults under 70 kilograms (11 stone). All lessons are held in either the outdoor manege or the indoor arena – both are floodlit.

BR West Dulwich

❑ 3, P4, S11, 115

££

Lee Valley Riding Centre

Lea Bridge Road, Leyton, E10 (0181 556 2629)

Classes are available for children and adults on twenty-one horses and ponies. There is an outdoor floodlit manege and an indoor riding arena, a cross-country course and paddock classes, as well as limited hacking.

⊖ Leytonstone

❑ W13, W14, W15, W16, 66, 145, 230, 257

££

London Equestrian Centre

Lullington Garth, Finchley, N12 (0181 349 1345)

This school has forty horses to suit all shapes, sizes and standards. If you have never ridden here before, you will be assessed before you are put into a class to check your ability. Lessons take place in a large, covered arena, and an outdoor manege. Jump lessons are also available and there are field rides in the summer.

⊖ Mill Hill East

❑ 221, 240

££

Manor Farm Livery Stables

Petersham Road, Richmond, Surrey TW10 (0181 940 8511)

Jump lessons and side-saddle lessons are available here in addition to regular teaching and hacks. There are fourteen horses, an outdoor manege and a livery yard.

⊖/**BR** Richmond

❑ H22, 33, H37, R61, 65, R68, R69, R70, 190, 290, 337, 371, 391, 415, 427

££

Mottingham Farm Riding Centre

Mottingham Lane, SE9 (0181 857 3003)

The grounds here cover 16 hectares (40 acres), with a cross-country course and a stream, and all lessons are held outdoors. Features include special ladies-only group riding lessons. Lessons are available only to people under 83 kilograms (13 stone).

BR Mottingham

❑ 124, 126, 161

££

Mudchute Park and Farm Riding School

1 Pier Street, Isle of Dogs, E14 (0171 515 0749)
See also page 102
A small riding school and part of Mudchute City Farm, this is a particularly good place for children (over seven years old) to get basic riding instruction, as well as to familiarize themselves with farm animals.
DLR Mudchute
❑ D6, D7, D8, D9, P14
££

Richard Briggs Riding Stables

63 Bathurst Mews, W2 (0171 723 2813/706 3806)
The fun of riding in Hyde Park makes the hair-raising trip along Bayswater Road from the stables beforehand worthwhile. There are twelve horses in this school and as well as riding in the park, you can have lessons in the two outdoor maneges or small indoor arena.
⊖ Marble Arch
❑ 2, 6, 7, 10, 12, 15, 16, 16A, 23, 30, 36, 73, 74, 82, 94, 98, 135, 137, 137A, 274
££

Ross Nye's Riding Establishment

8 Bathurst Mews, W2 (0171 262 3791)
Basic riding instruction is available here, with sixteen horses to choose from, and the chance to ride along Hyde Park's Rotten Row. There is also a children's pony club.
⊖ Marble Arch
❑ 2, 6, 7, 10, 12, 15, 16, 16A, 23, 30, 36, 73, 74, 82, 94, 98, 135, 137, 137A, 274
££

Snaresbrook Riding School

67–69 Hollybush Hill, Snaresbrook, E11 (0181 989 3256)
This school caters specifically for the family and weekend rider, with plenty of classes for adults and children in an indoor arena or an outdoor manege.
⊖ Snaresbrook
❑ W12, W13, W14
££

Suzanne's Riding School

Brookshill Farm, Brookshill Drive, Harrow Weald, Middlesex (0181 954 3618)
This riding school is lucky enough to have 81 hectares (200 acres) of grassland to ride on, including a cross-country and show-jumping course, three outdoor and one all-weather arena. There are fifty-three horses in the senior school and about thirty in the junior school.
⊖ Stanmore
❑ H12, 107, 142, 340
££

Willow Tree Riding Establishment

Ronver Road, Hither Green, SE12 (0181 857 6438)
There are about forty horses here and lessons are held in either an indoor arena or an outdoor manege. The school also caters for riders with special needs.
BR Grove Park, Lee
❑ 126, 136, 261, 284
££

Wimbledon Village Stables

24 Wimbledon Village High Street, SW19 (0181 946 8579)
All riding takes place outdoors on Wimbledon Common, where there's an outdoor ring. Hacking, jumping and dressage lessons are also available, plus two-hour rides to Richmond Park. Indoor classes take place too.
⊖ Wimbledon
❑ 57, 93, 131, 155, 156, 163, 164, 200
££

The recognized bodies are:

The British Horse Society, British Equestrian Centre, Stoneleigh, Kenilworth, Warwickshire CV8 2LR (01203 696697)

The Riding for the Disabled Association, Avenue R, National Agricultural Centre, Kenilworth, Warwickshire CV8 2LY (01203 696510)

ROWING

Rowing is an extremely popular sport amongst Londoners and there are plenty of clubs to choose from, most of which welcome beginners. Contact the Amateur Rowing Association (see below) for details; they also provide information on rowing facilities and regattas for the disabled.

As to spectating, see page 188.

The recognized body is:

Amateur Rowing Association, 6 Lower Mall, W6 9DG (0181 741 7580)

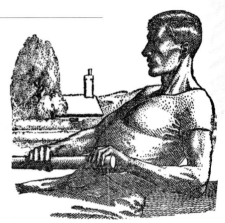

RUGBY LEAGUE

Contact the London Amateur Rugby League, which can direct you to your local club. Matches are played throughout London between September and May.

The recognized body is:

London Amateur Rugby League, 6 Queensmere Close, SW19 5NZ (0181 947 6119)

RUGBY UNION

Matches are played throughout London every weekend during the winter. Contact the London Division of the Rugby Football Union to find your nearest club.

As to spectating, Twickenham (see below for address) is London's major venue for home internationals, internationals and finals of club, county and divisional competitions. The main season runs from October to March and during the week you can take the RFU tour. For more details contact the Tours Manager on 0181 892 8161. Tours take place by appointment.

BR Twickenham, Whitton

❑ H22, 281

££

The recognized body is:

Rugby Football Union, RFU Ground, Whitton Road, Twickenham, Middlesex (0181 892 8161)

RUGBY AT TWICKENHAM BY TRAM FROM HAMMERSMITH OR SHEPHERDS BUSH

SKIING

London may not have any mountains, but there are plenty of artificial ski slopes where you can practise your snow ploughs before going on holiday.
Alexandra Palace Ski Centre, Alexandra Park, N22 (0181 888 2284)
Crystal Palace National Sports Centre, Ledrington Road, SE19 (0181 778 8600)
Hillingdon Ski Centre, Park Road, Uxbridge, Middlesex UB10 9NH (01895 255183)

SOFTBALL

Softball is one of the fastest growing sports of the past few years and today there are hundreds of amateur teams which play throughout the summer in London's parks. All you need are a handful of people, a bat and a ball and you are away. A word of warning though: it is first come, first served for space and the central London parks can get very overcrowded on a warm summer's evening, so make sure you arrive early. Alternatively, phone your local borough council to find out if they have any official softball pitches which you can book in advance. In this way, if your team plays regularly in a league, you can have your own home pitch on which to play.

The recognized body is:
National Softball Federation, Flat 3, Netherall Gardens, Hampstead, NW3 5TP (0171 435 6781)

SWIMMING

Listed below are the main outdoor pools in alphabetic borough order. Charges vary and will be approximately the same as your local public indoor pool.

CAMDEN

Hampstead Mixed Bathing Pond
East Heath Road, Parliament Hill, NW5 (0171 485 4491)
One of three ponds available (see next two entries). These ponds contain natural (and therefore cold) water, are free to use and are a wonderful alternative to chemically treated swimming pools. Changing rooms are available.

BR Gospel Oak, Hampstead Heath

❑ C11, C12, 24, 46, 168

Open: May–mid September; must be competent swimmer; no children under fifteen

Highgate Bathing Pond

Highgate Road, Parliament Hill Fields, NW5 (0171 485 4491)
This is Hampstead Heath's men-only pond. It is free and changing rooms are available.
BR Hampstead Heath

❑ C11, C12, 24, 46, 168

Open: all year; must be competent swimmer; no children under fifteen

Kenwood Ladies Pond

Hampstead Lane, Highgate, N6 (0171 485 4491)
The third of Hampstead Heath's ponds, this one is for women only. As with the others, it is free and changing rooms are available.
BR Gospel Oak, Hampstead Heath

❑ C11, C12, 24, 46, 168

Open: all year; must be competent swimmer; restrictions for children under sixteen

Oasis Sports Centre

32 Endell Street, WC2 (0171 831 1804)
You can swim comfortably all year round in the outdoor heated pool here. It is part of a leisure centre with an indoor pool and cafeteria too.
θ Covent Garden, Holborn

❑ 1, 8, 14, 19, 22B, 24, 25, 29, 38, 55, 68, X68, 91, 98, 168, 171, 176, 188, 501, 502, 521

Open: daily, 7.30 a.m.–8.30 p.m.
£

Parliament Hill Lido

Off Gordon House Road, Parliament Hill, NW5 (0171 485 4491)
This is a chlorinated outdoor swimming pool. Refreshments are available too.
BR Gospel Oak

❑ C11, C12

Open: May–late September, 7.00 a.m.–dusk

LAMBETH

Brockwell Lido

Brockwell Park, Dulwich Road and Norwood Road, Herne Hill, SE24 (0181 674 6141)
Following an impressive facelift, Brockwell Lido has reopened after a four-year closure. As well as the pool, there is a day nursery, fitness classes and rooms available for party hire.
θ Brixton
BR Herne Hill

Open: late May–September, 7.00 a.m.–dusk

Tooting Bec Lido

Tooting Bec Lido Road, Tooting, SW16 (0181 871 7198)
The second largest pool in Europe, Tooting Bec Lido is 92 metres (100 yards) long! Refreshments are available all through the summer too.
⊖/BR Tooting Bec
❑ 249, 319
Open: late May–September, 10.00 a.m.–7.30 p.m.
£

WESTMINSTER

Serpentine Lido

Hyde Park, W2 (0171 724 3104)
See also page 45
Located in Hyde Park in the heart of London, the Serpentine Lido is a unique place to swim and sunbathe. The pool features facilities to help disabled people and there are also plenty of poolside activities, including table tennis.
⊖ Knightsbridge, South Kensington
❑ C1, 9, 10, 14, 19, 22, 45A, 49, 52, 70, 74, 137, 137A
Open: May–September, 8.00 a.m.– dusk
£

The recognized body is:
The Amateur Swimming Association, Harold Fern House, Derby Square, Loughborough LE11 0AL (01509 230431)

WATERSPORTS CENTRES

The following centres offer a variety of watersports, including canoeing, sailing, windsurfing and power-boat racing. Weekends are the busiest times for these centres and they are often closed for a day during the week. Opening times vary depending on the time of year and the weather, so it is best to phone first.

BARNET

Welsh Harp Youth Sailing Base

Cool Oak Lane, West Hendon, NW9 (0181 202 6672)
Part of Barnet Council's Youth Service programme, the Welsh Harp Youth Sailing Base is open for children and adults between nine and twenty-five years of age. There are proficiency courses and young people work towards British Canoe Union and Royal Yacht Association certificates. Trips away are occasionally organized too.
Activities: canoeing, sailing, waterskiing
BR Hendon
❑ 32, 83, 142, 183
££

The Pirate Club Water Activities Centre

Oval Road, Camden, NW1 (0171 267 6605)
The Pirate Club is open to young people between the ages of eight and twenty-one. For the younger members the emphasis is on fun, while older members can train to a high degree of proficiency.
Activities: canoeing
⊖ Camden
❏ C2, 24, 27, 29, 31, 134, 135, 168, 214, 253, 274
££

Southmere Educational Boating Centre

Binsey Walk, Thamesmead, SE2 (0181 310 2452)
Part of Greenwich Community College, Southmere is the centre for the nautical studies department. Courses are available on a wide range of subjects, including skippering. Most courses are four weeks long, others are two terms and are for all ages and abilities.
Activities: canoeing, navigation, sailing, skippering windsurfing
BR Greenwich
❏ B11, 180, 272, 401, 469
££

Islington Boat Club

16–34 Graham Street, N1 (0171 253 0778)
Catering for young people between nine and eighteen years old, this club offers a wide choice of activity, including regular trips away (as far as Europe) and courses to help improve proficiency.
Activities: boating, canoeing, sailing
⊖ Angel
BR Farringdon, Old Street
❏ 4, 19, 30, 38, 43, 73, 141
££

Albany Park Sailing Centre

Albany Park Road, Albany Mews, Kingston upon Thames, Surrey KT1 (0181 549 3066)
This centre is open to anyone over the age of eight. Adult courses tend to be held on Tuesday and Thursday evening, and other weekday nights are set aside for the youth club. Disabled people are welcome too.
Activities: canoeing, sailing
BR Kingston
❏ K1, K2, K3, K4, K5, K6, 57, 65, 71, 85, 111, 131, 213, 281, 285, 371, 406, 465, 479
££

Lee Valley Watersports Centre

Greaves Pumping Centre, North Circular Road, Chingford, E4 (0181 531 1129)
See also page 37
Open all year, this centre caters for all ages from eight and some activities are suitable for disabled people too. Sailing courses are offered at weekends, as well as basic instruction in windsurfing. Immediate-level instruction in power-boating is also available.

The centre offers the Royal Yacht Association Young Sailors scheme and racing courses.
Activities: canoeing, power-boating, sailing, waterskiing, windsurfing
BR Highams Park
❑ 34, 444
££

Leaside Young Mariners Youth Club

Spring Lane, Upper Clapton, E5 (0181 806 6887)
Based alongside the River Lea, this club has been running for over thirty years and offers courses on canoeing and mountain-biking up to the standards of their governing bodies. It also provides leisure activities to local schools and youth groups, as well as school holiday, weekend and evening activities.
Activities: sailing
BR South Tottenham, Stamford Hill
❑ 106, 253

NEWHAM

Docklands Watersports Club

King George V Dock, Woolwich Manor Way, North Woolwich, E16 (0171 511 5000)
Mostly used at weekends by adults, school children have the chance of riding pillion on jet skis during the school holidays.
Activities: jet-skiing
DLR Beckton
❑ 69, 101, 473
££

RICHMOND

Thames Young Mariners

Ham Fields, Riverside Drive, Nr Richmond, Surrey TW10 (0181 940 5550)
Multi-activity courses are available during the school holidays, including orienteering and mountain-biking. The centre caters for students from beginners to advanced level and runs Royal Yacht Association and British Canoe Union courses all year round. Trips away are occasionally organized too.
Activities: canoeing, kayaking, power-boating, sailing, windsurfing
Ө/BR Richmond
❑ 65, 371
££

Surrey Docks Watersports Centre

Rope Street, Off Plough Way, Rotherhithe, SE16 (0171 237 4009)
This centre caters for all ages and abilities, including people with special needs. Children can either enjoy the activities for fun or train to gain British Canoe Union and Royal Yacht Association-approved certificates. Parents can join in too, and on Sunday you can go along to brush up your skills in one-off training sessions.
Activities: canoeing, power-boating, raft-racing, sailing, windsurfing
⊖ Surrey Quays
❑ P11, 47, 188, 199, 225
££

Docklands Sailing Centre

Kingbridge, Millwall Dock, E14 (0171 537 2626)
Open all year, on Saturdays there are special events and courses, while on Sundays anyone can come and join in. Courses on offer include power-boat instructor courses, shore-based courses, yacht, coastal and ocean master courses, as well as training in skippering, electronic navigation and diesel maintenance. School holiday activities include a 'Youth Afloat' programme run in conjunction with other centres.
Activities: canoeing, dragon-boat-racing, rowing, sailing, windsurfing, as well as angling, bungee-jumping and sub-aqua activities
DLR Crossharbour, Mudchute
❑ D5, D6, D8, D9
££

Westminster Boating Base

Dinorvic Wharf, 136 Grosvenor Road, Westminster, SW1 (0171 821 7389)
Royal Yacht Association and British Canoe Union courses are held here for adults and children. The base also hires out marquees for receptions and parties.
Activities: canoeing, power-boating, sailing
⊖ Pimlico
❑ 2, C10, 24, 36, 77A, 88, 185
££
    The recognized bodies are:
British Canoe Union, John Dudderidge House, Adbolton Lane, West Bridgford, Nottingham NG2 5AS (01602 821100)
British Canoe Union – Greater London and South East, 14 Reeves Avenue, Kingsbury, NW9 8LP (0181 205 5388)
British Water Ski Federation, 390 City Road, EC1 (0171 833 2855)
The Cruising Association, Ivory house, St Katharine's Dock, E1 (0171 481 0881)
Royal Yachting Association, RYA House, Romsey Road, Eastleigh, Hampshire SO5 4YA (01703 629962)
Thames Valley Yachting Association, 6 Courtlands Avenue, Hampton TW12 3NT (0181 979 1019)

❖

SPORTS FOR THE DISABLED

Sport is available at all levels for disabled people in London, with more facilities opening every year. Listed below are the main organizations responsible for promoting sport for the disabled.

LOCAL AUTHORITIES

Each London borough has a department responsible for the provision of facilities for sport and recreation in its area. Many boroughs have sports development officers responsible for encouraging participation in sport by under-represented 'target groups' such as disabled people. Contact the Leisure or Recreation Department of your borough for information on policies and provisions.

VOLUNTARY ORGANIZATIONS

British Sports Association for the Disabled
London Regional Manager, BSAD - Greater London Region, Solecast House, 13/27 Brunswick Place, N1 6DX (0171 490 4919)
BSAD develops and co-ordinates sport and physical recreation for disabled people. The London office can tell you about local sports clubs and events and organizations which specialize in a particular sport.

Greater London Association of Disabled People
336 Brixton Road, SW9 7AA (0171 274 0107)
GLAD is the representative voice of disabled Londoners with a membership of twenty-eight borough-based disability organizations and nine further organizations of disabled people.

United Kingdom Sports Association
Secretary, 30 Philip Lane, Tottenham, N15 4JB (0181 885 1177)
The UK Sports Association is a national charity providing services for people with a mental handicap. It also acts as a co-ordinating body in the provision of sports facilities and organizes some regional events.

SPECIALIST ORGANIZATIONS

Listed below are a number of voluntary organizations which specialize in sports provision for particular groups of disabled people or in making opportunities to take part in particular sports available to disabled people.

British Blind Sports
67 Albert Street, Rugby, Warwickshire CB21 2SN (01788 536142)
Promotes sports facilities and events for blind people, including rambling and swimming.

British Deaf Sports Council

7A Bridge Street, Otley, Yorkshire LS21 1BQ (01943 850214)
Promotes sports facilities and events for deaf people, including badminton, billiards, darts, football and golf.

British Ski Club for the Disabled

Corton House, Corton, Nr Warminster, Wiltshire BA12 0SZ (01985 850321)
This ski club organizes special ski trips for the disabled throughout the winter months.

The British Wheelchair Sports Foundation

c/o Jean Stone, Harvey Road, Stoke Mandeville, Buckinghamshire HP21 8PP (01296 84848)
Lots of sporting activities are organized by this foundation, at national and international level, including archery, athletics, basketball and fencing.

CP Sport – Spastics Society

11 Churchill Park, Colwick, Nottingham NH4 2HF (01159 401202)
Events are on a regional, national and international level. Sports catered for include athletics, football and swimming.

Great Britain Wheelchair Piscatorial Association

76 Leicester Road, Failsworth, Manchester M35 0QP (01424 427931)
Free national information centre for disabled people who are interested in fishing.

Jubilee Sailing Trust

Test Road, Eastern Docks, Southampton SO1 1GG (01703 638625)
An organization which encourages sailing for disabled people.

Riding for the Disabled Association

Avenue R, National Agriculture Centre, Kenilworth, Warwickshire CV8 2LY (01202 696510)
A large organization which promotes horseriding for disabled people of all ages.

Uphill Ski Club

12 Park Crescent, London W1N 4EQ (0171 636 1989)
Skiing for people of all disabilities is organized by this club. They have a centre in Scotland and arrange regular trips to Austria and Colorado.

Wheelchair Paraplegic Fencing Association

London and North East Area, Vera Burge, 24 Orchard Avenue, New Malden, Surrey KT3 4OT (0181 942 1725)
Open to people with any type of disability, including blindness. Weekend training sessions are held at Stoke Mandeville.

Overleaf: *Fireworks after the Lord Mayor's Show*

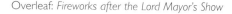

OUTDOOR
ENTERTAINMENT

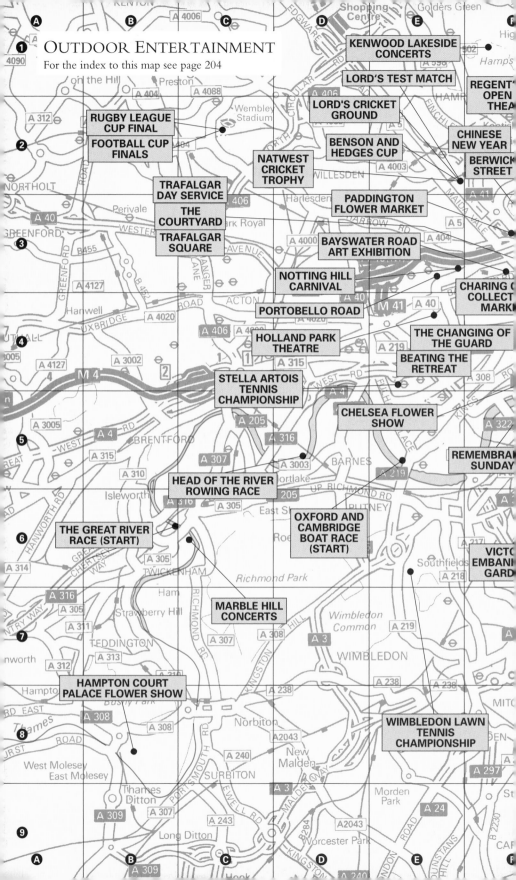

OUTDOOR ENTERTAINMENT

For the index to this map see page 204

KENWOOD LAKESIDE CONCERTS

LORD'S TEST MATCH

LORD'S CRICKET GROUND

REGENT'S OPEN THEA

RUGBY LEAGUE CUP FINAL

FOOTBALL CUP FINALS

BENSON AND HEDGES CUP

CHINESE NEW YEAR

NATWEST CRICKET TROPHY

BERWICK STREET

TRAFALGAR DAY SERVICE

THE COURTYARD

TRAFALGAR SQUARE

PADDINGTON FLOWER MARKET

BAYSWATER ROAD ART EXHIBITION

NOTTING HILL CARNIVAL

CHARING C COLLECT MARK

PORTOBELLO ROAD

THE CHANGING OF THE GUARD

HOLLAND PARK THEATRE

BEATING THE RETREAT

STELLA ARTOIS TENNIS CHAMPIONSHIP

CHELSEA FLOWER SHOW

REMEMBRA SUNDAY

HEAD OF THE RIVER ROWING RACE

OXFORD AND CAMBRIDGE BOAT RACE (START)

VICTO EMBAN GARD

THE GREAT RIVER RACE (START)

MARBLE HILL CONCERTS

HAMPTON COURT PALACE FLOWER SHOW

WIMBLEDON LAWN TENNIS CHAMPIONSHIP

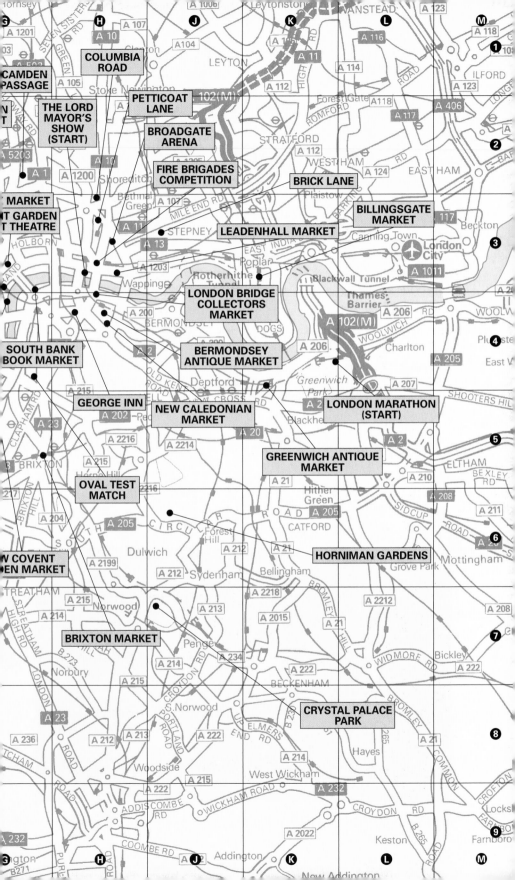

9
THEATRE AND CONCERTS

L ONDON is famous for its West End theatres and shows, but there is plenty of entertainment – from Shakespeare to alternative comedy – outdoors. Several of the larger parks put on a season of plays in purpose-built open-air theatres during the summer, while buskers and street entertainers offer something a little more offbeat.

OUTDOOR THEATRE

Covent Garden Street Theatre
WC2
Just round the corner from the prestigious, but expensive, Royal Opera House you can watch all sorts of budding performers for free. From clowns and dancers to musicians and mime artists, the variety is endless. Although the entertainment is officially free, performers are allowed to ask for money and, as this is often their only source of income, please support them by digging deep into your pockets!
Performances: daily
Θ Covent Garden
❑ 14, 19, 24, 29, 38, 176
Donations welcome

Street musician, Covent Garden

❖

George Inn

77 Borough High Street, SE1 (0171 407 2056)
See also page 177
The George Inn is a beautiful galleried coaching inn which was used regularly by Charles Dickens, and has close connections with William Shakespeare. On 23 April, St George's Day and Shakespeare's birthday, one of Shakespeare's plays is always performed in the courtyard outside the pub. Other plays are put on during the summer season on an irregular basis. Look out for posters or phone for details. Morris dancers also perform here some evenings and weekends during the summer.
Performances: phone for details
⊖ London Bridge
❏ D1, P3, D11, P11, 17, 21, 22A, 35, 40, 43, X43, 47, 48, 133, 344, 501, 521

Holland Park Theatre

Holland Park, Kensington High Street, W8 (0171 602 7856: Box Office; 0171 603 1123: Information)
See also page 13
The summer programme includes opera, dance and theatre.
Performances: June–mid-August, 7.30 p.m. or 8 p.m.; phone for details
⊖ High Street Kensington, Holland Park
❏ 9, 9A, 10, 27, 28, 31, 49, 52, 70, 94
££

Regent's Park Open-air Theatre

Inner Circle, Regent's Park, NW1 (0171 486 2431: Box Office)
See also page 49
The programme alternates between two Shakespearian productions and one other play (either a musical or modern classic) throughout the summer. Food is served before the show, as well as coffee and other refreshments during the interval which you can take into the performance. The bar stays open afterwards until midnight.
Performances: May–September, 7.45 p.m., Monday–Saturday; matinée performance at 2.30 p.m. on Wednesday, Thursday and Saturday
⊖ Baker Street, Great Portland Street, Regent's Park
❏ 2, C2, 13, 18, 27, 30, 74, 82, 113, 135, 139, 159, 274
££

OUTDOOR CONCERTS

As well as regular performances by the royal military bands in the royal parks, there are many open-air venues scattered across London where all types of music are performed.

'Music's strain can sweetly soothe'

BANDS IN THE PARKS

Royal Parks Band Performances
Greenwich Park, Hyde Park, Regent's Park and St James's Park
See also pages 45–54
A regular programme of music is put on in these parks during the summer, with plenty of traditional tunes to enjoy.
Performances: mid-afternoon to early evening, daily
⊖ see individual entry for each park
Performances are free, though normal deckchair charges apply

Broadgate Arena
Corner of Liverpool Street and Eldon Street, EC2 (0171 588 6565: information)
The centrepiece of the Broadgate Centre, Broadgate Arena has become a popular artistic and cultural oasis in the heart of the City. There is entertainment here throughout the year and a programme of events attracting people from all over the city. In the winter the arena is flooded and frozen to become London's only open-air ice rink (see also page 133). From April onwards, the space is used for lunchtime programmes of theatre, dance and music.
Performances: weekday lunchtimes
BR/⊖ Liverpool Street
❑ 8, 11, 22A, 22B, 23, 35, 42, 43, 47, 48, 78, 100, 133, 141, 149, 172, 214, 271, 243A

Crystal Palace Park
SE20 (0181 778 7148)
See also page 30
Summer concerts run during July and August. Phone for details of each concert, its cost and to make advance bookings.
Performances: Sundays
⊖ Brixton
BR Crystal Palace
❑ 2, 3, 63, 122, 137A, 157, 202, 227, 249, 306, 322, 352, 358, 450

❖

Victoria Embankment Gardens

Villiers Street, WC2 (0171 828 8070)
Between the end of May and the first week of August, daily lunchtime concerts take place in these gardens. There is also a short opera season during June and July, with performances taking place three or four nights a week (see also page 15).

Performances: concerts May–August lunchtimes, daily;
opera: June–July, three to four nights a week

⊖ Embankment

❏ 3, 6, 9, 11, 12, 15, X15, 23, 24, 29, 53, X53, 77A, 88, 91, 94, 109, 139, 159, 176

Horniman Gardens

100 London Road, Forest Hill, SE23 (0181 699 2339)
See also page 30
Concerts take place during July and August. During the school holidays there are shows for children on Tuesdays and Thursdays. Phone for details.

Performances: Sundays

BR Forest Hill

❏ 122, 176, 185, 194, 312

Kenwood Lakeside Concerts

Kenwood House, Hampstead Lane, NW3
(0171 413 1443: Box Office)
See also page 118
The elegant grounds of Kenwood House provide an imposing backdrop to these popular concerts which attract audiences from all across London. On some evenings the music is accompanied by dazzling firework displays.

Performances: July–early September every Saturday evening (you are advised to book well in advance)

⊖ Archway, Golders Green

❏ 210

££

Marble Hill Concerts

Marble Hill House, Richmond Road, Twickenham, Middlesex TW7 (0171 943 3426)
See also pages 71 and 119
Regular concerts take place in the grounds of this beautiful Palladian villa every Sunday between mid-July and early September. The concerts offer mostly classical music, with the last concert of the season usually a jazz night. Strict parking restrictions are enforced, so it is sensible to take public transport, unless you have booked a parking space (limited) within the grounds.

⊖ Richmond
BR St Margaret's
❏ H22, 33, H37, R68, R70, 90, 290
££

10
MARKETS

SHOPPING in markets is much more fun than pushing a trolley up and down supermarket alleys – and you might find some bargains too. Choose from antiques, clothes, food, and household goods or simply browse and enjoy the crowded and lively atmosphere.

Alongside favourite haunts, such as Portobello Road and Petticoat Lane, there are a large number of local markets which are an excellent place to buy household goods and fruit and veg.

Wholesale markets are interesting to visit, if you don't mind getting up very early in the morning. Once sited in the heart of London, many have been moved to the outskirts, but they still retain their unique atmosphere. Check out Billingsate for fish, Borough and New Covent Garden for flowers, fruit and veg, and, if you're not squeamish, Smithfield for meat. A word of warning though – these markets are for wholesalers who buy in bulk, so don't expect to come home with a couple of pork chops or a piece of smoked salmon!

CAR BOOT SALES

Boot sales are the latest addition to outdoor trading and are extremely popular. Taking place every weekend in all sorts of locations, from school playgrounds to wasteland and fields, they provide an excellent way to sell off your own junk, as well as to rummage through other people's to find the occasional bargain.

As venues for boot fairs change so regularly, it is impossible to list them here. The best way to find out where your nearest one takes place is to read *Car Boot Monthly* (a bi-monthly publication) or your local newspaper.

HOW TO FIND A MARKET

The markets are listed below in alphabetic order, with information regarding opening hours and access by public transport. Opening times are only approximate: stall-holders are licensed to trade between certain hours but obviously they decide how long to trade within that time. As a general rule, the earlier you arrive the better.

Bayswater Road Art Exhibition
Bayswater Road, W2
Over 250 artists and craftspeople sell their own original work at the world's longest open-air art show. Best to arrive at lunchtime.
⊖ Lancaster Gate, Queensway
❑ 12, 94
Open: Sunday, 9.00 a.m.–6.00 p.m., including Easter Sunday

Bermondsey Antique Market

Corner of Long Lane and Bermondsey Street, SE1
You need to arrive very early (no later than 5.00 a.m.) to catch the bargains here, and remember to bring a torch! This market is particularly popular with antique dealers, who will buy in bulk to sell on elsewhere.
⊖/**BR** London Bridge
❑ 1, 42, 78, 188, 199
Open: Friday, 4.00 a.m.–2.00 p.m.

Berwick Street

W1
Stretching through the heart of Soho, this market is always busy with shoppers and has plenty of choice. Worth buying here is fish, and you should also be able to find fresh herbs and unusual fruit and vegetables too. Busiest at lunchtime.
⊖ Oxford Circus
❑ C2, 3, 6, 7, 8, 10, 12, 13, 15, 16A, 23, 25, 53, 55, 73, 88, 94, 98, 113, 135, 137, 137A, 139, 159, 176
Open: Monday–Saturday, 9.00 a.m.–5.00 p.m., including Good Friday, bank holiday Mondays; closed 25 and 26 December

Billingsgate Market

North Quay of West India Dock, Isle of Dogs, E14
Billingsgate moved here in 1982, from its site on the edge of the City. Most fish is sold in bulk, but you may find some traders prepared to make an exception.
DLR West India Quay
❑ D6, D7, D8, 330
Open: Tuesday–Saturday, 5.00 a.m.–8.30 a.m.

Berwick Street Market

Brick Lane

E1

Brick Lane is an area lived in by a mix of races and religions, and this cosmopolitan atmosphere is reflected in its lively market. Buy a bagel from one of several bakeries *en route* and enjoy browsing through the bargains, bicycles and junk you will find.

⊖/**BR** Liverpool Street

⊖ Aldgate East

❑ 8, 11, 22A, 22B, 23, 26, 35, 42, 43, 47, 48, 78, 100, 133, 141, 149, 172, 214, 243A, 271

Open: Sunday, 8.00 a.m.–1.00 p.m., including Easter Sunday

The Brick Lane clothes show
Nearest Station Aldgate East

Brixton Market

SW9

Brixton's most famous road, Electric Avenue, which later became the subject for a song by reggae star Eddy Grant, is the central vein of this market, which also runs along Popes Road and Brixton Station Road. Reggae and other music provide a background accompaniment to shopping here, with ghetto blasters blaring out from nearby record shops and stalls.

⊖/**BR** Brixton

❑ 2, 3, P4, P5, 35, 37, 45, 45A, 109, 133, 159, 196, 250, 322

Open: Monday–Tuesday and Thursday–Saturday, 9.00 a.m.–5.30 p.m.; Wednesday, 9.00 a.m.–1.00 p.m., including Good Friday, 24 and 31 December; closed other bank holidays

Camden Market

Camden High Street, NW1

If you don't mind the crowds, especially on weekends, Camden Lock is one of the most exciting and enjoyable markets to visit in London. The market starts just outside Camden underground station and spreads up the high street to the lock and beyond. There is an enormous range of stalls, selling everything imaginable, and as it does tend to get very busy, it is worth coming early, so you'll be able to enjoy it more.

⊖ Belsize Park, Camden Town, Chalk Farm

❑ C2, 24, 27, 29, 31, 134, 135, 168, 214, 253, 274

Open: Monday–Friday, 10.00 a.m.–5.00 p.m.; Saturday and Sunday, 9.00 a.m.–6.00 p.m., including Easter Sunday, all bank holiday Mondays and 24 December

Camden Passage

N1

An important point to know about Camden Passage before setting off from home is that it is in Islington, not Camden – it was named after the Earl of Camden. The market is set in a narrow passage behind Upper Street and comprises a

Camden Market

variety of antiques stalls tucked outside the antique shops already there.
⊖ Angel
❑ 4, 19, 30, 38, 43, 56, 73, 153, 171A, 214, 279
Open: Wednesday, 6.45 a.m.–4.00 p.m. (antiques); Thursday, 7.00 a.m.–4.00 p.m.
(books, prints and drawings); Saturday, 8.00 a.m.–5.00 p.m. (antiques); closed
26 December

Charing Cross Collectors' Market
Junction of Northumberland Avenue and Embankment Place, WC2
This is a specialist market, where collectors of coins, antiquities, banknotes, bonds
and stamps gather to buy and sell. It is a fascinating and unusual market and well
worth a visit, even if you're not a collector.
⊖/BR Charing Cross
⊖ Embankment
❑ 3, 6, 9, 11, 12, 13, 15, 23, 24, 29, 53, 77A, 88, 91, 94, 109, 139, 159, 176
Open: Saturday, 8.00 a.m.–3.30 p.m.

Columbia Road
E2
Whether you're a professional horticulturist or just a weekend gardener, this is the
place to go to snap up some wonderful plants, garden fittings and equipment.
Flowers are a major, and colourful, feature here, as well as crafts, and it is unlikely
you will go home empty-handed.
⊖/BR Liverpool Street
❑ 5, 22A, 22B, 26, 35, 43, 47, 48, 55, 67, 78, 149, 243, 243A
Open: Sunday, 7.00 a.m.–2.00 p.m., including Easter Sunday

The Flower Market by Tube

Sunday mornings at Columbia Road, Shoreditch
Nearest stations: Old Street, Shoreditch

Columbia Road Flower Market by Kay Gallwey
One of a series commissioned by London Underground

The Courtyard

St Martin-in-the-Fields, WC2

Over 250 designer/makers and artists sell their work from forty stands all year round. It is a particularly good place to hunt for Christmas presents, with an enormous selection of ceramics, jewellery, glass, clothing and other individual gifts.

⊖/**BR** Charing Cross

❏ 3, 6, 9, 11, 12, 13, 15, 23, 24, 29, 53, 77A, 88, 91, 94, 109, 139, 159, 176

Open: Monday–Saturday, 11.00 a.m.–6.00 p.m.; Sunday, 10.00 a.m.–4.00 p.m., including bank holiday Mondays; closed Good Friday, Easter Sunday, 25 and 26 December

Covent Garden – Apple Market

Covent Garden, WC2

Once the home of London's fruit and vegetable market, Covent Garden is now one of the city's most famous shopping areas. The Apple Market is located under the glass roof of the central market building and here you will find a selection of crafts, toys and jewellery.

⊖ Covent Garden

❏ 14, 19, 24, 29, 38, 176

Open: daily, 9.00 a.m.–7.00 p.m. (antiques Sunday and Monday; crafts Tuesday–Saturday); closed 25 and 26 December

Earlham Street

WC2

This is a small market, where you find antiques, books, records, clothes and cut flowers. Best in the week.

⊖ Covent Garden

❏ 14, 19, 24, 29, 38, 176

Open: Monday–Saturday, 12 a.m.–6.00 p.m.; closed bank holidays

Gabriel's Wharf

56 Upper Ground, SE1 (on the South Bank between the National Theatre and the Oxo Tower)

This wharf was renovated about twenty years ago and has more recently become a lively market area with stalls selling jewellery, sculpture, textiles, ceramics, toys, fashion and restored antiques. There are also several restaurants and sandwich bars.

⊖/**BR** Waterloo

❏ 1, D1, 4, D11, P11, 26, 68, 76, 77, 149, 168, 171, 171A, 176, 188, 211, 501, 505, 507, 521

Open: Tuesday–Sunday, 11.00 a.m.–6.00 p.m. (extra market every Friday, 11.00 a.m.–3.00 p.m.)

Greenwich Antique Market

Burney Street, SE10

Greenwich's market is rapidly becoming as popular as Camden's. Its popularity has inevitably pushed prices up, so you are unlikely to find any bargains in the

❖

antiques section, but it is still worth a browse.
BR Greenwich
❑ 177, 180, 188, 199, 286, 386
Open: Saturday and Sunday, 8.00 a.m.–4.00 p.m., including Easter Sunday

Leadenhall Market
Gracechurch Street, EC3
An elaborate Victorian market arcade built of cast-iron and stone, this is a popular market with city workers at lunchtime. The best buys here are game, poultry, fish, meat and cheese.
⊖ Bank, Monument
❑ 8, D9, 11, 15, 15B, X15, 17, 21, 22A, 22B, 23, 25, 26, 35, 40, 43, X43, 47, 48, 76, 133, 149, 501
Open: Monday–Friday, 9.00 a.m.–5.00 p.m.; closed bank holidays and 24 December

London Bridge Collectors' Market
London Bridge Station, SE1
A covered market with sixty-five stalls, selling collectables – coins, stamps, medals, militaria, postcards, antiquities.
⊖/**BR** London Bridge
❑ D1, P3, D11, P11, 17, 21, 22A, 35, 40, 43, X43, 47, 48, 133, 344, 501, 521
Open: Saturday, 7.30 a.m.–3.30 p.m.

National Film Theatre South Bank Book Market
South Bank, SE1 (underneath Waterloo Bridge)
Books and crafts are sold here alongside the river. Buskers perform here too, particularly in summer.
⊖/**BR** Waterloo
❑ 1, D1, 4, D11, P11, 26, 68, X68, 76, 77, 149, 168, 171, 171A, 176, 188, 211, 501, 505, 507, 521
Open: Saturday and Sunday and most weekdays, 12 a.m.–dusk, including Easter Sunday; also Good Friday and all bank holiday Mondays

New Caledonian Market
Bermondsey Square, E1
Main market for antique dealers. Best to come mid-morning.
⊖/**BR** London Bridge
❑ 1, 42, 78, 188, 199
Open: Friday, 6.00 a.m.–2.00 p.m., including Good Friday

New Covent Garden Market
Nine Elms Lane, SW8
The fruit and vegetable market moved here in 1974 from its original Covent Garden site. Today it is in less elegant surroundings but it is busier than ever. Although the vegetable section does not particularly welcome visitors, the flower market is more friendly, and it is possible to buy single trays of plants and smallish bunches of flowers.

⊖/BR Vauxhall
❏ 44, 344
Open: Monday–Friday, 3.30 a.m.–10.30 a.m.

New Covent Garden Sunday Market
Nine Elms Lane, SW8
General goods.
⊖/BR Vauxhall
❏ 44, 344
Open: Sunday, 9.00 a.m.–2.00 p.m., including Easter Sunday

Paddington Flower Market
North Wharf Road, W2
Flowers, plants, pots, garden furniture, house plants, shrubs, trees, dried flowers.
⊖/BR Paddington
⊖ Edgware Road, Warwick Avenue
❏ 7, 23, 27, 36, 70
Open: Sunday, 10.00 a.m.–4.00 p.m., including Easter Sunday

Petticoat Lane

Middlesex Street, E1
Petticoat Lane is one of the most famous streets in London, with its enormous market packed with over 1,000 stalls on a Sunday. All sorts of goods are offered here, from kitchen gadgets sold by noisy and entertaining microphone salesmen to second-hand clothes and bric-à-brac.
Θ/**BR** Liverpool Street
ΘAldgate, Aldgate East
❏ 8, 11, 22A, 22B, 23, 26, 35, 42, 43, 47, 48, 78,100, 133, 141, 149, 172, 214, 243A, 271
Open: Sunday, 9.00 a.m.–2.00 p.m., including Easter Sunday; closed 25 December

Piccadilly Market

Forecourt of St James's Church, 197 Piccadilly, W1
A small market away from the hurly-burly of Piccadilly, here you will find arts, crafts, antiques, bric-à-brac, jewellery and knitwear.
Θ Green Park, Piccadilly
❏ 3, 6, 8, 9, 12, 14, 15, 19, 22, 23, 38, 53, X53, 88, 94, 139, 159
Open: Friday and Saturday, 9.30 a.m.– 6.00 p.m.; closed Good Friday, Easter Saturday

Portobello Road

W11
Winding its way down through the back of Notting Hill, this market is famed throughout the world for its antiques. Silver, prints, furniture, ceramics and collectables are all offered here, at high prices.

The flea market is where you are more likely to find a bargain. Although, traditionally, not as smart as the top end of the road, the stalls here sell good-quality items, such as kitchenware and collectable ceramics, as well as modern household goods, second-hand clothes and records.
Θ Notting Hill Gate, Ladbroke Grove
❏ 7, 23, 52, 70, 302
Open: antiques (junction with Westbourne Grove to Colville Terrace) Saturday, 7.00 a.m.–5.00 p.m.; *general market* (Colville Terrace to Thorpe Close) Monday–Wednesday, 8.00 a.m.–5.00 p.m.; Thursday, 8.00 a.m.–1.00 p.m.; Friday and Saturday, 8.00 a.m. – 6.00 p.m. or earlier, including Good Friday, 24 and 31 December; closed public holidays; *flea market* (Thorpe Close to Golborne Road) Friday and Saturday, including Good Friday, 8.00 a.m.– 6.00 p.m. (best before dusk); closed public holidays

Smithfield Market

EC1
This world-famous meat market is the last wholesale market to remain on its original site. The market is located in an impressive cast-iron building designed by Horace Jones to keep the place cool and well aired, and has rejected modern automation in favour of its traditional white-coated porters, who heave the carcasses around in trolleys.
Θ Barbican, Farringdon
❏ 55, 56, 63, 153, 243, 259, 279, 505
Open: Monday–Friday, 5.00 a.m.–10.30 a.m.

11
EATING AND
DRINKING

IN THE past few years eating and drinking outside have finally caught on, as Londoners have begun to realize that you don't need Mediterranean sunshine to be able to enjoy an outdoor lifestyle. Areas in the heart of the city, such as Covent Garden (largely a pedestrian area) and Charlotte Street (with its wide pavements) are particularly well suited to alfresco eating and have numerous streetside cafés and restaurants. With its narrow pavements and busy streets, Soho is less suited, but if you don't mind the traffic fumes and the noise, choose a seat on the street and enjoy this area's colourful bustle and activity.

As well as streetside cafés and restaurants, London has a wealth of other alfresco eateries to suit all pockets and tastes, from the elegant Belvedere restaurant in the heart of Holland Park and the popular Dukes Head pub on Putney's riverside, to the charms of Cannizaro House in Wimbledon, where you can enjoy afternoon tea in beautiful surroundings.

Outer London has good places where you can eat and drink outdoors too. Down by the river, Richmond's waterfront has several watering holes, while many pubs, such as the Hand in Hand Wimbledon and the Cricketer's Arms in Mitcham, have a wonderful, rural atmosphere yet are only a few miles from the city centre.

To whet your appetite, listed below are the pick of the bunch across London. Each entry includes practical information on opening times and transport. Easy parking near these restaurants and pubs cannot be guaranteed in central London, but further afield it should be easier.

Bon Appetit!

RESTAURANTS

CENTRAL

Barbican Waterside Café
Level 5, Barbican Centre, EC2 (0171 638 4141)
If you've just visited the Barbican's glorious conservatory (see page 115), the Waterside café, with its attractive lake and fountains, makes an excellent place to stop for refreshment.
⊖ Barbican, Moorgate
❑ 4, 21, 43, X43, 56, 76, 133, 141, 172, 214, 271
Open: 10.00 a.m.–8.00 p.m.

Café des Amis du Vin

11–14 Hanover Place, WC2 (0171 379 3444)

Set in a tiny, narrow alley, this charming wine bar and restaurant could easily be overlooked. Not recommended if you want a good view, but ideal for a quiet and atmospheric romantic dinner or if you're going to the Royal Opera House, which is just round the corner.

⊖ Covent Garden

❑ 14, 19, 24, 29, 38, 176

Open: 12 a.m.–11.30 p.m.

Café Flo

51 St Martin's Lane, WC2 (0171 379 0314)

This Café Flo, close to Trafalgar Square and the National Gallery, is one of a chain of stylish cafés across London. You can go for a meal or just a coffee or a drink. They all have outside seating, as much as space allows.

⊖ Leicester Square

❑ 14, 19, 24, 29, 38, 176

Open: Monday–Friday 9.00 a.m.–11.30 p.m.; Saturday and Sunday, 9.00 a.m.–10.30 p.m. Also at:

334 Upper Street, N1 (0171 226 7916)
205 Haverstock Hill, NW3 (0171 435 6744)
149 Kew Road, Richmond, Surrey (0181 940 8389)
127–129 Kensington Church Street, W8 (0171 727 8142)
676 Fulham Road, SW6 (0171 371 9673)

Café Rouge

36–48 James Street, W1 (0171 487 4847)

There are plenty of tables outside this French-style café (one of several Café Rouges across London). It is a good place to go for a meal, or simply for a coffee or drink.

⊖ Bond Street

❑ 6, 7, 8, 10, 12, 13, 15, 16A, 23, 73, 94, 98, 113, 135, 137, 137A, 139, 159

Open: Monday–Saturday 10.00 a.m.–11.00 p.m.; Sunday; 12 a.m.–5.00 p.m. Also at:

27–31 Basil Street, Knightsbridge, SW3 (0171 584 2345)
10 Cabot Square, Canary Wharf ,E14 (0171 537 9696)
227–229 Chiswick High Road, Chiswick, W4 (0181 742 7447)
30 Clifton Road, Maida Vale, W9 (0171 286 2266)
15 Frith Street, Soho, W1 (0171 437 4307)
855 Fulham Road, Fulham, SW6 (0171 371 7680)
19 High Street, Hampstead, NW3 (0171 433 3404)
Hay's Galleria, Tooley Street, SE1 (0171 378 0097)
2 Lancer Square, Kensington Church Street W8 (0171 938 4200)
200 Putney Bridge Road, Putney, SW15 (0181 788 4257)
291 Sandycombe Road, Kew, TW9 (0181 332 2882)

❖

Chez Gérard

8 Charlotte Street, W1 (0171 636 4975)

Charlotte Street has become one of the main centres of upmarket alfresco eating in London. Chez Gérard, which serves French food, is one of the best restaurants at which to sit outside, as it is on the sunny side of the street.

θ Tottenham Court Road

❑ 7, 8, 10, 14, 19, 22B, 24, 25, 29, 38, 55, 73, 98, 134, 176

Open: Sunday–Friday, 12 a.m.–3.00 p.m., 6.00 p.m.–11.00 p.m.; Saturday, 5.30 p.m.–11.00 p.m.

Soho Brasserie

23–25 Old Compton Street, W1 (0171 439 9301)

One of the best vantage points in Soho to watch the world go by. Open from mid-morning to late at night, this is a popular haunt for trendy media types.

θ Tottenham Court Road

❑ 7, 8, 10, 14, 19, 22B, 24, 29, 38, 55, 73, 98, 134, 176

Open: Daily 10.00 a.m.–11.30 p.m.

NORTH

Anna's Place

90 Mildmay Park, N1 (0171 249 9379)

One of the few restaurants in London specializing in Swedish food, Anna's Place, a popular local Islington venue, has a garden with five tables.

θ Highbury & Islington

❑ 73

Open: Tuesday–Saturday, 12.15 p.m.–2.15 p.m., 7.15 p.m.–11.45 p.m.

Casale Franco

134–137 Upper Street, Islington N1 (0171 226 8994)

This popular Italian restaurant boasts one of the most unusual settings. It is opposite a car repair workshop, so it can be quite noisy during the day. In the evenings, when the workshop has closed, you can sit outside in the small courtyard.

θ Angel, Highbury & Islington

❑ 4, 19, 30, 43, X43

Open: Tuesday–Sunday, 12.30 p.m.–2.30 p.m., 6.30 p.m.–11.30 p.m.

SOUTH

Le Pont de la Tour

Butler's Wharf Building, 36d Shad Thames, Butler's Wharf, Bermondsey, SE1 (0171 403 8403)

A glamorous restaurant overlooking the Thames, Le Pont de la Tour is the most expensive of four restaurants along this part of the riverbank, all owned by restaurateur and designer Terence Conran. The other three, all a stone's throw apart and with a number of outdoor tables, are:

❖

Blue Print Café
Design Museum, Butler's Wharf, Bermondsey, SE1 (0171 378 7031)
The Butler's Wharf Chop House
Butler's Wharf Building, 36e Shad Thames, Bermondsey, SE1 (0171 403 3403)
Cantina del Ponte
Butler's Wharf Building, 36c Shad Thames, Bermondsey, SE1 (0171 403 5403)
⊖ Tower Hill
❑ P11, 42, 47, 78, 188
Open: all restaurants have different opening times; please phone for details

National Film Theatre Café

South Bank, Waterloo SE1 (0171 828 5362)

This is a good-value, self-service restaurant with plenty of large outdoor tables. There is plenty to do nearby (the NFT is part of the thriving South Bank Centre).

⊖/**BR** Waterloo
❑ 1, D1, 4, D11, P11, 26, 68, X68, 76, 77, 168, 171, 171A, 176, 188, 211, 501, 505, 507, 521
Open: 10.00 a.m.–9.00 p.m.

WEST

Café Lazeez

93/95 Old Brompton Road, South Kensington, SW7 (0171 581 9993)

Café Lazeez is an attractive restaurant with several outdoor tables. The food is Indian and the atmosphere is decidedly trendy.

⊖ South Kensington
❑ C1, 14, 45A, 49, 70, 74
Open: Monday–Saturday 11.00 a.m.–1.00 a.m.; Sunday, 11.00 a.m. –11.00 p.m.

Canal Brasserie

222 Kensal Road, Kensal Green, W10 (0181 960 2732)

Close to the Grand Union Canal, the brasserie has outdoor seating in an attractive whitewashed yard full of pots of flowers and a pretty fountain.

⊖ Ladbroke Grove, Westbourne Park
❑ 23, 28, 31, 52, 70, 295, 302
Open: Monday–Thursday, 9.30 a.m.–3.00 p.m., 7.00 p.m.–1.00 a.m.; Friday, 9.30 a.m.–3.00 p.m., 7.00 p.m.–2.00 a.m. (closed at weekends, but available for private hire)

Feng Shang Restaurant

15 Prince Albert Road, London, NW1 (0171 485 8137)

This is a stationary restaurant, moored on Regent's Park Canal. There is a gangway leading to the bridge from Prince Albert Road.

⊖ Camden Town
❑ 24, 274
Open:Monday - Friday 12 noon - 2 p.m., 6 p.m. - 11 p.m. Saturday and Sunday 12 noon - 11 p.m.

Any park or open green space provides an opportunity for a picnic. The trick is to find your favourite site and note where it is so you can find it next time! Most parks have refreshment facilities of some sort, even if it is just an ice-cream vendor, but some parks have cafés and restaurants which are so good they are worth mentioning in their own right. Here are some of the best, listed alphabetically, and I have also included cafés in public gardens or attached to historic houses, where you can sit and have afternoon tea in the most attractive of surroundings.

The Belvedere

Holland Park, off Abbotsbury Road, Holland Park, W8 (0171 602 1238)
Without doubt, this is the smartest place to eat in any park in London. The restaurant is set in the heart of Holland Park and has five tables on the terrace outside. (See also page 13.)
⊖ Holland Park
❏ 94

Open: Monday–Saturday, 12 a.m.–2.30 p.m., 6.00 p.m.–10.45 p.m.; Sunday, 12 a.m.–3.00 p.m.

Cannizaro House

West Side, Wimbledon Common, SW19 (0181 879 1464)
A beautiful hotel, where you can sit and have tea on the terrace overlooking the gardens. (See also page 116.)
BR Wimbledon
❏ 93, 200
P Parking area
Open: 3.00 p.m.–6.00 p.m. for tea

Chelsea Physic Garden

Royal Hospital Road, Chelsea, SW3 (0171 351 5646)
The Chelsea Physic Garden was founded in 1673 by the Apothecaries' Company for the collection, study and dissemination of plants and is one of Europe's oldest botanic gardens. It has a lovely café, with a good choice of homemade food, but you will have to pay to enter the garden even if you just want to have tea. (See also page 110.)
⊖ Sloane Square
❏ 239

Open: April–October, Wednesday–Saturday, 2.00 p.m.–5.00 p.m.
£

Clissold Park Café

The Mansion, Clissold Park, Stoke Newington Church Street, Stoke Newington, N16 (0171 249 0672)
In a Grade II listed building, this is a family-friendly café with plenty of hearty teatime cakes and biscuits. (See also page 20)
⊖ Manor House
❏ 73, 106, 141, 171A

Open: 10.00 a.m.–7.00 p.m.

Golders Hill Park Cafeteria

North End Way, Golders Hill, NW3 (0181 455 8010)
Just down the road from its big brother, Hampstead Heath, this small but pleasant park boasts its own bandstand and a delightful café run by an Italian family who have decorated it with baskets and tubs of colourful flowers.
⊖ Golders Green
❑ 210, 268
Open: 10.30 a.m.–9.00 p.m.

Ham House

Ham, Surrey TW10 (0181 940 1950)
Set in an orchard in the grounds of the recently restored Ham House, this is a lovely setting to enjoy a light lunch or tea. (See also page 117.)
⊖/**BR** Richmond
❑ 65, 371
Open: Tuesday–Sunday, 10.00 a.m.–5.00 p.m.

Kenwood House Café

The Old Stables, Kenwood House, Hampstead Lane, Hampstead, NW3 (0181 348 1286)
There is a café and restaurant in the beautiful old Coach House at Kenwood House, where you can have tea and snacks or a wholesome and filling lunch. (See also page 118.)
⊖ Archway, Golders Green
❑ 210
Open: May–September, 10.00 a.m.–6.00 p.m.; October–April, 10.00 a.m.–4.00 p.m.

Kew Gardens

Kew, Surrey, TW9
Kew Gardens has three eateries, offering a wide enough range of food and drink to suit all hungry horticulturists, from the elegance of the Orangery, the smartest of the three, to the convenience of the self-service Pavilion and Bakery cafés. (See also page 113.)
⊖/**BR** Kew Gardens
❑ 65, R68, 391
The Orangery (0181 948 1825)
Open: mid-March–December, 10.00 a.m.– dusk
The Pavilion (0181 940 7177)
Open: October–March, 10.00 a.m.– 4.00 p.m.; April–September, 10.00 a.m.– 5.30 p.m. Monday–Saturday, to 7.00 p.m. Sunday
Kew Bakery (0181 332 1138)
Open: 10.00 a.m.– closing time

Lauderdale House

Waterlow Park, Highgate Hill, Highgate, N6 (0181 341 4807)
Lauderdale House, a restored Grade I listed building, is now home to a small art gallery and a café. You can take your food out on to the terrace overlooking the park below. (See also page 26.)

⊖ Archway
❑ 210
Open: Tuesday–Sunday, 9.00 a.m.–6.00 p.m.

Neal's Lodge
Wandsworth Common, Off Baskerville Road, Wandsworth, SW18 (0181 870 7484)
Located close to the common's bowling green and cricket pitch, Neal's Lodge has a wonderful peaceful atmosphere. You can have drinks on the patio first and then move to the conservatory to eat and enjoy looking out at the view.
BR Wandsworth Common
❑ C1, 115, 219, 249, 319
Open: Tuesday–Sunday, 12.30 p.m.–2.30 p.m.; Tuesday–Saturday, 6.30 p.m.–11.30 p.m.

Oshobasho Café
Highgate Woods, Muswell Hill Road, N10 (0181 444 1505)
Formerly a cricket pavilion, Oshobasho Café is now a successful vegetarian restaurant and, unlike most park cafés, it is licensed.
⊖ Highgate
❑ 43, X43, 134, 263
Open: Tuesday–Sunday, 8.30 a.m.–7.00 p.m.

Nightingales Restaurant
Petersham Hotel, Nightingale Lane, Richmond, Surrey TW10 (0181 940 7471)
Nightingales Restaurant is one of the best vantage points to appreciate the beautiful view across Petersham water meadows to the winding River Thames. After lunch, why not step into the view and walk along the riverside.
⊖/**BR** Richmond
❑ 65, 371
Open: 12.30 p.m.–2.30 p.m., 6.30 p.m.–11.30 p.m.

Pembroke Lodge
Richmond Park, Surrey TW10 (0181 940 8207)
Close to the Richmond entrance to the park, Pembroke Lodge offers afternoon tea and snacks in its own grounds within the park.
⊖/**BR** Richmond
❑ 65, 371
Open: March–October, 10.00 a.m.–½ hour before park closes; November–February, 10.00 a.m.–4.00 p.m.

Ritz
150 Piccadilly, W1 (0171 493 2687)
The hotel's restaurant has wonderful views across to Green Park and in the summer it is possible to sit outside in the beautiful Italian Garden.
⊖ Green Park
❑ 8, 9, 14, 19, 22, 38
Open: 12.00 p.m.–3.00 p.m., 6.30 p.m.–11.30 p.m.

PUBS

Opening times vary from pub to pub and also depend on the season. The general rule in England is that they are open from 11.00 a.m. and closed by 11.00 p.m.

Sitting outside means you can bring the children along to the pub too.

CENTRAL

The PS Tattershall Castle

Victoria Embankment, WC2 (0171 839 6548)

This paddle steamer is a former ferry that used to work on the Humber. Today, it is moored on the opposite bank to the Jubilee Gardens and upriver from Cleopatra's Needle and has open-air decks from where you can enjoy views across to the South Bank Centre.

Food available at lunchtimes and evenings.

⊖ Embankment

❑ 3, 6, 9, 11, 12, 13, 15, X15, 23, 24, 29, 53, X53, 77A, 88, 91, 94, 109, 139, 159, 176

The TS Queen Mary

Victoria Embankment, WC2 (0171 240 9404)

Moored close to Waterloo Bridge, this boat is a turbine steamer with bars, restaurants and open-air decks.

Food available at lunchtimes and evenings.

⊖ Embankment

❑ 1, 4, 6, 9, 11, 13, 15, 15B, X15, 23, 26, 68, X68, 76, 77A, 91, 168, 171, 171A, 176, 188, 501, 505, 521

NORTH

The Canonbury Tavern

21 Canonbury Place, Islington, N1 (0171 226 1881)

The most unusual feature of this pub is its petanque (French bowls) court. There is also room to sit and drink outside too.

Food available at lunchtimes and evenings (not Sunday).

⊖ Highbury & Islington

❑ 43, 143, 263

The Freemasons Arms

32 Downshire Hill, Hampstead, NW3 (0171 435 4498)

Large pub near Hampstead Heath, which is very busy at weekends.

Food available at lunchtimes only.

BR Hampstead Heath

❑ C11, C12, 24, 46, 168, 268

The Green Dragon

889 Green Lanes, Winchmore Hill, N21 (0181 360 2374)

There is a large pleasant garden at the back of this pub, which features an unusual

children's 'fantasy tree' climbing frame.

Food available at lunchtimes and evenings.

⊖ Winchmore Hill

❏ W2, 329

The Rising Sun

137 Marsh Lane, Mill Hill, NW7 (0181 959 3755)

In the garden of this pub, you will find a 400-year-old oak tree. The pub is nearly as old too.

Food available at lunchtimes and evenings, with regular barbecues in the summer.

BR Mill Hill Broadway

❏ 113, 186, 251

SOUTH

The Anchor

Bankside, 34 Park Street, Southwark, SE1 (0171 407 1577)

Close to William Shakespeare's Globe Theatre and the Clink prison, the Anchor is in the heart of one of the most historically interesting areas of London. Next to the river, it has a large riverside patio with plenty of tables, and looks across to Hungerford Bridge and the City.

Food available at lunchtimes only.

⊖ London Bridge

BR Cannon Street

❏ D1, P3, D11, P11, 17, 21, 22A, 35, 40, 43, X43, 47, 48, 133, 344, 501, 521

The Crown and Greyhound Hotel

73 Dulwich Village, Dulwich, SE21 (0181 693 2466)

Close to Dulwich Park, this is a large family pub, which is particularly popular at Sunday lunchtime. There is a large grassy garden, away from the road, where children can play safely, and a conservatory for when it rains.

Food available at lunchtimes and evenings (not Sunday).

BR North Dulwich

❏ P4, S11

The Cutty Sark Tavern

Ballast Quay, Greenwich, SE10 (0181 858 3146)

An attractive late sixteenth-century building, the Cutty Sark Tavern in Greenwich has good views across to the Isle of Dogs, from a terrace outside on a narrow cobbled lane.

Food available at lunchtimes and evenings.

BR Maze Hill

DLR Island Gardens, then by foot tunnel

❏ 177, 180, 286

❖

The Dukes Head

8 Lower Richmond Road, Putney, SW15 (0181 788 2552)
There's a great view over to Bishop's Park from this riverside pub, and it is also a good spot from which to watch the Oxford and Cambridge Boat Race, which starts from nearby Putney Bridge (see page 188).

Food available at lunchtimes only.

☻ Putney Bridge

❑ 14, 22

The Founders Arms

Bankside, 52 Hopton Street, Southwark, SE1 (0171 928 1899)
This pub was built in 1980 on the site of the foundry that cast the bell for St Paul's. The pub is modern and basic inside, but has a nice atmosphere and plenty of room to appreciate the views across to the City.

Food available at lunchtimes and evenings.

☻ Blackfriars

❑ P11, 45, 63, 172

The George Inn

77 Borough High Street, Borough, SE1 (0171 407 2056)
(See also page 153)
The George Inn was a popular haunt of both William Shakespeare and Charles Dickens. It has a huge courtyard, where occasional jousts, Morris dancing and Shakespeare plays are performed.

Food available at lunchtimes and some evenings.

☻ Borough, London Bridge

❑ D1, P3, D11, P11, 17, 21, 22A, 35, 40, 43, 47, 48, 133, 344, 501, 521

The Hand in Hand

6 Crooked Billet, Wimbledon, SW19 (0181 946 5720)
Next to Wimbledon Common, this pub is a particular favourite on summer weekends. If you arrive any later than noon, you will be unlikely to find a table in the attractive courtyard outside the pub. There is also a children's play area.

Food available at lunchtimes and evenings.

☻/BR Wimbledon

❑ 93, 200

The George Inn

The Mayflower

117 Rotherhithe Street, Rotherhithe, SE16 (0171 237 4088)
The eighteenth-century Mayflower pub has a small riverside jetty, with excellent views across to Wapping and Docklands. The pub takes its name from the Pilgrim Fathers' ship, which sailed from here in 1611.
   Food available lunchtimes and evenings (not Monday evening).
⊖ Rotherhithe
❑ P11, 255

The Old Thameside Inn

Clink Street, Southwark, SE1 (0171 403 4243)
At lunchtime on the last Sunday of every month, the London Shantymen perform sea shanties here. The riverside terrace offers great views across to the City too.
   Food available at lunchtimes only.
⊖/**BR** London Bridge
❑ D1, P3, D11, P11, 17, 21, 22A, 35, 40, 43, X43, 47, 48, 133, 344, 501, 521

The Ship Inn

41 Jews Row, Wandsworth, SW18 (0181 870 9667)
Part of an old dock area, now converted to offices, the Ship Inn has a large terrace overlooking the river. A Thames barge is moored alongside and the terrace has plenty of outdoor tables and benches to accommodate everyone when it gets busy – as it always does on summer evenings.
   Food available at lunchtimes and weekends, with barbecues in the summer.
BR Wandsworth Town
❑ C3, 28, 44, 295

The Sun Inn

7 Church Road, Barnes, SW13 (0181 876 5256)
Situated in a picturesque spot across the road from Barnes Pond, this pub has several tables in a small garden at the front of the pub. Beware, though: they get snapped up very fast, so try to arrive early.
   Food available at lunchtimes only.
BR Barnes
❑ 9, 9A, 33, R69, 72

The Trafalgar Tavern

Park Row, Greenwich, SE10 (0181 858 2437)
A popular pub down by the river in Greenwich which first opened in 1836 and was a favourite with Charles Dickens.
   Food available at lunchtimes and evenings (Tuesday–Saturday).
BR Greenwich
DLR Island Gardens, then by foot tunnel
❑ 177, 180, 188, 286, 386

The Windmill Inn

Windmill Drive, South Side, Clapham Common, SW4 (0181 673 4578)

❖

> ### The Trafalgar Tavern
>
> An inn on the site of the present Trafalgar Tavern was first recorded in the eleventh century, when is was thought to have been known as the George Tavern. Located in the heart of Greenwich, it has always been closely associated with the Royal Navy and, at one time, provided living quarters for sailors.
>
> In the nineteenth century, the tavern became a favourite haunt of the famous English writer Charles Dickens (1812–70), who mentions it in his book *Our Mutual Friend*.
>
> The present building was erected in the nineteenth century, in 1837, by the architect Joseph Kay, who also worked on the nearby Greenwich Hospital.

Adjacent to the common, this pub has two patios with picnic tables (one has a colonnaded shelter too) and a children's play area. Extremely busy on summer evenings because of its attractive setting, it is still an enjoyable pub to visit.

Food available at lunchtimes and evenings.

⊖ Clapham Common, Clapham South

❏ 60, 115, 155, 355

EAST

The Barley Mow

44 Narrow Street, Limehouse, E14 (0171 265 8931)

Once a dock master's house, today it is a pleasant pub with a decently sized fore-court with benches and tables giving southerly views across the Thames to Rotherhithe.

Food available at lunchtimes and evenings.

DLR Limehouse

❏ 5, 15, 15B, 40, 100

The Dickens Inn

St Katharine's Way, St Katharine's Dock, EC1 (0171 488 1226)

One of the oldest pubs in London and a handy place to stop for lunch if you are visiting Docklands.

Food available at lunchtimes and evenings.

⊖ Tower Hill

DLR Tower Gateway

❏ D1, D9, D11, 15, X15, 25, 42, 78, 100

The Dove

25–27 Broadway Market, Bethnal Green, E8 (0171 275 7617)

The Dove has a wonderful garden, which includes a fountain, as well as colourful flowerbeds.

Food available at lunchtimes and evenings (not Sunday).

⊖ Bethnal Green

❏ 26, 48, 55

The Dickens Inn

The Duke of Somerset
Little Somerset Street, City, E1 (0171 481 0785)
The Duke of Somerset is one of the only pubs in the City with a proper patio garden, which, although small and often crowded, is still pleasant.

Food available at lunchtimes only.

⊖ Aldgate

❑ D1, 5, D11, 15, 15B, X15, 25, 40, 42, 67, 78, 100, 253

The Falcon and Firkin
360 Victoria Park Road, Hackney, E9 (0181 985 0693)
This pub has a huge concreted garden next to Victoria Park. It is immensely popular and can become very busy in the summer.

Food available at lunchtimes only.

⊖ Mile End

❑ 277

The Prospect of Whitby
57 Wapping Wall, Wapping, E1 (0171 481 1095)
The Prospect of Whitby is the oldest pub in London, and dates from 1543, when it was known as the Devils' Tavern.
    Food available at lunchtimes only.
⊖ Tower Bridge
❑ 100

WEST

The Anglesea Arms
15 Selwood Terrace, South Kensington, SW7 (0171 373 7960)
An elegant, award-winning pub, its small forecourt is always crammed with people on summer evenings and weekend lunchtimes. Although on a fairly busy road, it retains a peaceful, relaxed atmosphere not always found in London pubs.
    Food available at lunchtimes only.
⊖ South Kensington
❑ 14, 45A, 211

The City Barge
Strand on the Green, Chiswick, W4 (0181 994 2148)
The City Barge is the second oldest pub on the Thames, dating from the sixteenth century, and is so close to the river it has floodgates. It also looks out across to Oliver's Island, where, in the seventeenth century, Oliver Cromwell once hid from the Cavaliers.
    Food available at lunchtimes and evenings.
⊖ Gunnersbury
❑ 7, 65, 237, 267, 391

The Cross Keys
Lawrence Street, Chelsea, SW3 (0171 352 1893)
At the back of this cosy pub is a small and pretty courtyard, decorated with lots of pots of flowers.
    Food available at lunchtimes only (not Sunday).
⊖ Sloane Square
❑ 239

The Dove
19 Upper Mall, Hammersmith, W6 (0181 748 9474)
Generally considered to be the nicest of all the pubs along this stretch of the river, the Dove is situated just above Hammersmith Bridge. It is a good place from which to watch the Oxford and Cambridge Boat Race (see page 188) and, on less busy days, to enjoy watching the oarsmen practise their strokes up and down the river.
    Food available at lunchtimes and evenings (not Sunday).
⊖ Ravenscourt Park
❑ 190

The Duke of Clarence

203 Holland Park, Holland Park, W8 (0171 603 5431)

This pub has an attractive, large conservatory and a flagged courtyard and is close to Holland Park.

Food available at lunchtimes and evenings (not Sunday).

⊖ Holland Park, Shepherd's Bush

❏ 94

The Fox

Green Lane, Hanwell, W7 (0181 567 3912)

Close to the Grand Union Canal, the Fox has a pleasant and grassy garden.

Food available at lunchtimes only.

BR Hanwell

❏ E1, E3, E4, E8, 83, 207, 607X

The Grange

Warwick Road, Ealing, W5 (0181 567 7617)

This pub on Ealing Common has a massive garden and conservatory. Hugely popular with locals, it can get pretty noisy on weekend evenings.

Food available at lunchtimes and evenings.

⊖ Ealing Common

❏ 207, 607

The Ladbroke Arms

54 Ladbroke Road, Notting Hill, W11 (0171 727 6648)

The prize-winning patio makes this an extremely attractive place to drink outside.

Food available at lunchtimes only.

⊖ Holland Park, Notting Hill Gate

❏ 12, 27, 28, 31, 52, 70, 94, 302

The Old Ship Inn

24 Upper Mall, Hammersmith, W6 (0181 748 3970)

This eighteenth-century pub which overlooks the Thames feels like an old ship inside, with its low ceilings and dark, cabin-like rooms.

Food available at lunchtimes and evenings.

⊖ Hammersmith.

❏ 27, H91, 190, 267, 290

The Orange Tree

Kew Road, Richmond, Surrey TW10 (0181 940 0944)

This pub has a tiny but picturesque patio, which can become very crowded.

Food available at lunchtimes and evenings (not Sunday).

⊖/**BR** Richmond

❏ 65, R68, 391

The White Cross

Richmond Riverside, Richmond, Surrey TW10 (0181 948 6767)

You can sit either outside in the garden at the front of the pub or inside to be able to enjoy the comings and goings along this attractive stretch of the Thames. Although there are several pubs along the riverside development in Richmond, this one is generally considered to be the best.

Food available at lunchtimes and evenings.

⊖/**BR** Richmond

❑ H22, 33, H37, R61, 65, R68, R69, R70, 90, 190, 290, 337, 371, 391

The White Horse

1 Parsons Green, Fulham. SW6 (0171 736 2115)

An extremely popular and often noisy pub, you can sit outside at tables over-looking Parsons Green.

Food available at lunchtimes and evenings.

⊖ Parsons Green

❑ C4, 22, 141

The White Swan

Riverside, Twickenham, Middlesex TW7 (0181 892 2166)

This is an idyllic seventeenth-century inn with a traditional pub atmosphere in a tiny back lane close to Marble Hill House. Its front garden runs down to the river along a peaceful stretch of the Thames.

Food available at lunchtimes and evenings, with a weekend barbecue in the summer.

BR Twickenham

❑ H22, 33, R68, R70, 90, 110, 267, 281, 290

The White Cross

12
THE LONDON YEAR

DOZENS of social, sporting and ceremonial events take place outdoors in London throughout the year and all are an important part of London life. The variety is endless, ranging from the traditional pomp and ceremony of Trooping the Colour in June, celebrating the Queen's official birthday, to Test Matches at Lord's Cricket Ground and the colourful Chinese New Year Festival in Soho.

They are all fun to watch and many are free. Some events described below may be familiar, but I have also included a selection of less well-known events to whet your appetite. Also, look in the local press for events such as flower shows, summer fêtes and fireworks displays near you.

PAGEANTRY

Throughout the year dozens of ceremonies take place all over London, many dating back hundreds of years and all forming part of Britain's tradition of pageantry. Royal pageantry undoubtedly makes the most impressive spectacle. Many events, such as the Changing of the Guard, were originally of military and political importance; the monarchs had to put on an impressive display of strength as a reminder of their power and authority to any potential enemy.

Less well-known are the displays of pageantry in the City, dating back to when merchants here were enormously powerful and effectively ruled the wealthy Port of London.

Throughout the year there are also traditional ceremonies which take place either to mark an important historical anniversary or to celebrate one of London's heroes or villains. All these events are listed below.

ROYAL CEREMONIAL EVENTS

The Ceremony of the Keys
Each evening, the gates of the Tower of London are locked by the Chief Warder of the Yeoman Warders, who is ceremonially challenged by a sentry as he nears the Bloody Tower. At 10.00 p.m. the Last Post is sounded and the Chief Warder hands over his keys to the Resident Governor and Major in the Queen's House. Applications to attend the ceremony must be made in writing at least two months in advance to Resident Governor, Resident Governor's Office, Ceremony of Keys, HM Tower of London EC3N 4AB.
⊖ Tower Hill
❑ 15, 25

The Mounting of the Guard

Horse Guards, Whitehall, SW1

The Mounting of the Guard takes place at the Horse Guards, opposite Whitehall at 11.00 a.m. on weekdays and 10.00 a.m. on Sundays. The guard is formed from two units of the Household Cavalry – the Blues (identified by the red plumes on their helmets) and the Life Guards (white-plumed).

⊖ Charing Cross, Westminster
BR Charing Cross
❑ 3, 11, 12, 24, 53, X53, 77A, 88, 109, 159

The Changing of the Guard

Buckingham Palace, SW1

The Queen's Guard, usually formed from one of the regiments of Foot Guards (the Scots, Irish, Welsh, Coldstream and Grenadier) is changed each morning at 11.30 a.m. The ceremony takes place inside the Palace railings and can be viewed by the public from outside. The Guard, usually accompanied by a band, leaves Wellington Barracks at 11.27 a.m. and marches via Birdcage Walk to the Palace. Between early April and September the ceremony takes place daily; from September to April it occurs on alternate days.

⊖/**BR** Green Park, St James's Park, Victoria
❑ 2, 8, 9, 11, 14, 16, 19, 22, 36, 38, 52, 73, 82

Horse Guards, Whitehall, SW1

The Queen's Life Guard is changed daily throughout the year at 11.00 a.m. from Monday–Saturday and 10.00 a.m. on Sundays. The ceremony lasts approximately twenty-five minutes. The Guard leaves Hyde Park Barracks at 10.28 a.m. (9.28 a.m. on Sunday) and rides via Hyde Park Corner, Constitution Hill and the Mall. Times may alter on days when state events are taking place. There is a short ceremonial dismounting of the mounted sentries every day at 4.00 p.m.

⊖ Charing Cross, Westminster
BR Charing Cross
❑ 3, 11, 12, 24, 88, 159, 176

St James's Palace, SW1

The St. James's Palace detachment of the Queen's Guard marches to Buckingham Palace at 11.15 a.m. and returns to St James's Palace at 12.10 p.m. The Guard is changed only on days when there is a Guard Change at Buckingham Palace.

⊖ Green Park, St James's Park
❑ 11, 24, 88, 211

Gun Salutes

Gun salutes take place annually on the following dates:

6 February	Ascension day
21 April	Queen's birthday
2 June	Coronation day
10 June	Prince Philip's birthday
4 August	Queen Mother's birthday

❖

No salute is ever fired on a Sunday, being held over to the next day if necessary. There is always a 41-gun salute at noon in Hyde Park, opposite the Dorchester Hotel, Park Lane, fired by the King's Troop, Royal Horse Artillery. The soldiers gallop their horses down through the park, pulling the massive gun carriages behind them, set them up, then fire.

A 62-gun salute is also fired at the Tower of London at 1.00 p.m. by the Honourable Artillery Company. Gun salutes also take place for Trooping the Colour and the State Opening of Parliament, as well as for some state visits – details for these vary.

Royal Mews

Buckingham Palace, SW1

The Royal Mews house the Queen's horses and the elegant carriages used on state occasions.

⊖/BR Victoria

❑ C1, 2, 8, C10, 11, 16, 24, 36, 38, 52, 73, 82, 185, 211, 239, 507

Open: late March–late September, Tuesday–Thursday, 12 a.m.–4.00 p.m.' early October–late March, Wednesday, 12 a.m.–4.00 p.m.

£

Annual Calendar of Social and Sporting Events

JANUARY/FEBRUARY

Lord Mayor of Westminster's New Year's Day Spectacular

This parade has been taking place for several years now and is a great way to start the year, with plenty to enjoy, from marching bands, floats and veteran cars, to horse-drawn carriages and clowns.

The event starts at noon on New Year's Day from Parliament Square and travels along Whitehall to Trafalgar Square, west along Cockspur Street and Pall Mall, north along Lower Regent Street to Piccadilly Circus, west along Piccadilly, north along Berkeley Street, finishing in Berkeley Square.

⊖ Green Park, Piccadilly, Westminster

❑ 3, 11, 12, 24, 53, X53, 77A, 88, 109, 159, 211

Charles I Commemoration

St. James's Palace, SW1

On 30 January 1649, King Charles I was beheaded. The commemoration of this event is held on the last Sunday in January by the King's Army (the Royalist wing of the English Civil War Society), dressed and armed in totally authentic seventeenth-century style. The march starts outside St James's Palace at 11.30 a.m. and makes its way down the Mall, through Horse Guards, to the Banqueting House, following the route of King Charles's last walk. Here, a short service of commemoration is held and a wreath is laid at noon beneath the window through which the king stepped on to the scaffold. This is followed by the presentation of the King's Army Service Awards and the Commissioning of Officers. The parade then marches up to Trafalgar Square, past the statue of Charles I, where a wreath has previously been laid, through Admiralty Arch and back down the Mall to St James's Palace, where the parade is dismissed.

For further information, phone the Banqueting House (0171 930 4179).

⊖ St James's Park

❏ 8, 9, 14, 19, 22, 38

Chinese New Year Festivities

Soho, WC2

London's Chinese community is based in Soho and the annual New Year celebrations are the highlight of their year. They are not held on a set date every year, because the Chinese calendar is lunar, and sometimes New Year will be in late January, at others in early February.

Chinese New Year

The area of Soho around Newport Place, Gerrard Street and Lisle Street comes alive from 11.00 a.m.–6.00 p.m. with decorations, streamers and garlands adorning windows and balconies. Among the most popular sights are the Lion Dances, when young men don colourful, theatrical lion costumes and weave their way through the streets, the 'lion' receiving gifts of money and food from residents, shops and restaurants en route.

Θ Leicester Square

❑ 14, 19, 38

MARCH/APRIL

Head of the River Rowing Race

0181 741 7580 (Amateur Rowing Association)

The Head of the River Race, on 20 March, is an exciting, crowded race for rowing boats from schools, universities and amateur clubs. Crews of eight, fours and sculls row the University Boat Race course, from Mortlake to Putney. The exact starting time varies according to tides and the race lasts about 1½hours. For the best view, stand on the Surrey bank above Chiswick Bridge. The Amateur Rowing Association organizes the Head and has details of local clubs and other local regattas and races around the country.

Θ Gunnersbury

BR Mortlake

❑ 9, 9A, 33, R69, 190, 290, 337, 415

Harness Horse Parade

Regent's Park, NW1 (0171 486 7095)

This annual parade of 200 working horses takes place on Easter Monday. Many different breeds are on show, from heavy shire horses and Somerset breeds to lighter-weight animals used for pulling commercial vans. Judging starts in the Inner Circle at about 9.30 a.m., with veterinary inspections followed by the main parade. Next comes the judging of a whole variety of categories from Heavy Horses, Single Horse Commercial Vans and Private Turnouts. Events end with a grand parade of winners from about noon until about 1.00 p.m.

Θ Baker Street, Great Portland Street, Regent's Park

❑ 2, 13, 18, 27, 30, 74, 82, 113, 139, 159, 274

Oxford and Cambridge Boat Race

Held in April, contact ARA for the date each year

The best-known rowing event of the year and, this is so popular that you might find it hard to see anything at all over the heads of all the other spectators! Oxford University and Cambridge University first raced each other from Hambledon Lock to Henley in 1829. The present course,

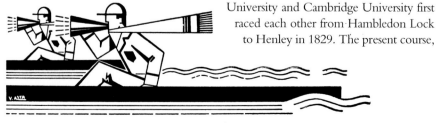

from Putney to Mortlake, was first used in 1845 and the race became an annual event in 1856. The most popular place from which to view the race is the finish at Mortlake.

There are other races which are equally enjoyable to watch (see above) and regattas are held regularly at Chiswick, Hammersmith, Kingston, Richmond and Twickenham. For details contact the Amateur Rowing Association, 6 Lower Mall, Hammersmith, W6 9DG (0181 741 7580).

⊖ Gunnersbury
BR Mortlake
❏ 9, 9A, 33, R69, 190, 290, 337, 415

London Marathon

Held in April, contact AAA for the date each year

See also page 127

Since the first London Marathon in 1980, this has become the world's largest road race, with over 35,000 starters. International runners lead the participants and behind come a mixture of serious runners, joggers, celebrities and fancy-dress fun-runners who raise thousands of pounds for charity. The two best places from which to watch are Greenwich, where it all starts at 9.30 a.m., and the finish at Westminster Bridge (approximately noon). The runners all appreciate some moral support, so you could just stand anywhere along the route and cheer them on! For details on entering the race phone the Amateur Athletics Association (0171 247 2963) or Sportsline (0171 222 8000).

⊖ Westminster (for finish)
DLR Island Gardens, then via foot tunnel (for start)
BR Greenwich (for start)
❏ 177, 180, 188, 199, 286, 366(start); D1, 3, 11, D11, P11, 12, 24, 53, X53, 76, 77, 77A, 88, 109, 171A, 159, 211, 507(finish)

Coca Cola Cup Football Final

Wembley Stadium, Stadium Way, Wembley, Middlesex (0181 900 1234: box office)

⊖/**BR** Wembley Central, Wembley Park
BR Wembley Stadium
❏ PR2, 83, 92, 182, 224, 226, 245, 297, 304
££

Tyburn Walk

St Sepulchre's, Newgate, Giltspur Street, EC4 (0171 248 1660: administrator)

At 3.00 p.m. on the last Sunday in April a group of Catholic worshippers walk from St Sepulchre's church to Hyde Park Corner, the site of the Tyburn gallows, where many Catholic martyrs, as well as prisoners, were put to death. The last execution there was in 1783; thereafter they took place at Newgate Prison, until it was demolished in 1868.

⊖ St Paul's
BR City Thameslink
❏ 8, 17, 22B, 25, 45, 46, 171A, 221, 243, 259, 501, 521

MAY

Rugby League Cup Final

Wembley Stadium, Stadium Way, Wembley, Middlesex (0181 900 1234: box office)
Θ/BR Wembley Central
BR Wembley Stadium
❑ PR2, 83, 92, 182, 224, 226, 245, 297, 304
££

One Day International Cricket Match

Lord's Cricket Ground, St John's Wood Road, NW8 (0171 289 8979: box office)
Θ St John's Wood
❑ 13, 82, 46, 113, 274
££

London to Brighton Cycle Ride

London Cycling Campaign, 3 Stamford Street, SE1 (0171 928 7220)
££ for entrants

FA Cup Final

Wembley Stadium, Stadium Way, Wembley, Middlesex (0181 900 1234: box office)
Θ/BR Wembley Central, Wembley Park
BR Wembley Stadium
❑ PR2, 83, 92, 182, 224, 226, 245, 297, 304
££

Chelsea Flower Show

Royal Chelsea Hospital, Hospital Road, SW3
Over four days, 4.5 hectares (11 acres) are given over to a mass of exhibitors showing everything for the green-fingered, from specially designed gardens and fruit and vegetable displays to garden equipment. Some plants and flowers on show may be sold to the public on the last day of the show. Postal applications for tickets to Chelsea Flower Show Ticket Office, PO Box 407, London SE11 5ET (0171 735 6199)
Θ Sloane Square
❑ 11, 137, 137A, 211, 239
££

The London Private Fire Brigades Competition

Guildhall Yard, EC2
The London Private Fire Brigade Association comprises sixty-six brigades, and since 1904 a competition involving target spraying has been staged in Guildhall Yard in the City. Teams of six, mostly all volunteers, compete for a Silver Challenge Shield, which is presented by the Corporation of London. One of the

penalties when the teams do not always keep the water jet under control is the soaking of onlookers!

For more details phone the information desk (0171 606 3030).

⊖ Bank, St Paul's

❑ 4, 8, D9, 11, 15, 15B, X15, 17, 23, 25, 26, 43, X43, 56, 76, 133, 149, 172, 501, 521

JUNE

Beating the Retreat

Horse Guards Parade, SW1 (0171 839 6815/6732: box office)

This is a popular military display of marching and drilling bands of the Household Division. There are mounted bands, trumpeters, massed bands and pipes and drums. Both the marching and drilling bands perform at 9.30 p.m., by floodlight. Tickets are available from the end of February from Premier Box Office, 1b Bridge Street, SW1 (opposite Big Ben).

⊖ St James's, Westminster

❑ 3, 11, 12, 24, 53, X53, 77A, 88, 109, 159

££

Later in the month is Sounding the Retreat, again in Horse Guards Parade, with massed band displays. Performances usually start at 7.30 p.m. and tickets are available by post from Headquarters, The Light Division, Sir John Moore Barracks, Winchester, SO22 6NQ.

⊖ St James's, Westminster

❑ 3, 11, 12, 24, 53, X53, 77A, 88, 109, 159

££

Trooping the Colour

This colourful ceremony marks the official birthday of the Queen and takes place at Horse Guards Parade in Whitehall on the second Saturday in June. Wearing the official uniform of one of the regiments of which she is Colonel-in-Chief, the Queen leaves Buckingham Palace at 10.30 a.m. to take the salute of the Brigade of Guards and the Household Cavalry. This is followed by a display of marching and the 'trooping' (display) of the 'colour' (or flag) of one of the regiments of Foot Guards.

C. LAWSON.

Trooping the Colour

The Queen arrives back at Buckingham Palace at 12.30 p.m. and appears on the balcony for a fly-past by the RAF at 1.00 p.m., when there is another gun salute at the Tower of London.

If you want to have a good viewpoint on the Mall to watch the parade you need to enter a ticket ballot, for which there is a small charge. For details write by the end of February to The Brigade Major (Trooping of the Colour), Household Division, Horse Guards Parade, SW1, enclosing a stamped-addressed envelope. There is a maximum of two tickets per application.

⊖ Charing Cross, St James's Park, Westminster
BR Charing Cross
❏ 3, 11, 12, 24, 53, X53, 77A, 88, 109, 159
££

Stella Artois Tennis Championships

Queen's Club, Palliser Road, W14 (0171 225 3733: box office)
Members of Queen's Club have priority for tickets for the championships, but the public can have a second bite at the cherry if they have put themselves on the mailing list (write to Stella Artois Tennis, c/o NABF, 189 Brompton Road, London SW3 1NE) before the end of the previous September. Otherwise, you can book for the remaining tickets by contacting the box office from the beginning of October.
⊖ Baron's Court
❑ C4, 28, 74, 190, 211, 295, 391
££

Lord's Test Match

Lord's Cricket Ground, St John's Wood Road, NW8 (0171 289 8979: box office)
⊖ St John's Wood
❑ 13, 46, 82, 113, 274
££

Wimbledon Lawn Tennis Championships

All England Lawn Tennis and Croquet Club, PO Box 98, Church Road, SW19 (0181 946 2244: recorded information)
One of the most popular sporting events in Britain, even when it rains, takes place during the last week of June and the first week of July. Seats for the Centre and No. 1 courts are allocated by public ballot (one application form per address), but you can queue for tickets for entry to other courts on the day of play. Play goes on into the early evening, especially during the first week, so try and pop along after work and you might be able to buy tickets for good seats at a discounted price from people who are leaving.

To enter the ballot, apply in writing for an application form to the All England Club between September and December, enclosing a stamped-addressed envelope.Completed forms must be returned by the end of January.
⊖ Southfields
⊖/**BR** Wimbledon
❑ 39, 93
££

The Knollys Red Rose Rent

Mansion House, EC4 (0171 606 3030: information)

In the fourteenth century Sir Robert Knollys was fined for building a footbridge over Seething (now part of the City) to join two of his properties. The fine was a nominal one – a red rose to be delivered to the Lord Mayor on Midsummer Day – and payment is still made by the Churchwarden of All Hallows-by-the-Tower, who carries the flower to the Mansion House on 24 June.

⊖ Mansion House

❑ 8, D9, 11, 15B, X15, 21, 22B, 23, 25, 26, 43, X43, 76, 133, 149, 501

££

JULY

Benson and Hedges Cup Final

Lord's Cricket Ground, St John's Wood Road, NW8 (0171 289 8979: box office)

⊖ St John's Wood

❑ 13, 46, 82, 113, 274

££

Doggett's Coat and Badge Race

(0171 606 3030: information desk)

Six Thames watermen row against the tide from London Bridge to Chelsea Bridge in late July or early August, and the winner is presented with a scarlet coat with silver buttons and badge. This is the oldest rowing event in the world, instituted in about 1715.

⊖/**BR** London Bridge (for start of race), Victoria (for finish of race)

❑ D1, P3, D11, P11, 17, 21, 22A, 35, 40, 43, X43, 47, 48, 133, 344, 501, 521 (for start of race)

Hampton Court Palace Flower Show

Hampton, Middlesex (0171 497 9955: ticket hotline)

See also page 110

Since the first show in 1990 this event has grown into one of the most important – and enjoyable – flower shows in Britain.

Covering 10 hectares (25 acres), there are always plenty of special attractions too, such as the British Rose Festival and exhibitions of endangered garden plants.

BR Hampton Court

❑ R68, 111, 131, 216, 415, 431, 440, 451, 461, 561, 572, 582, 726

〰launch from Westminster or Richmond

££

AUGUST

The Oval Test Match

The Oval, Kennington, SE11 (0171 582 6660: box office)

⊖ Oval

❑ 3, 36, 109, 133, 159, 185, 355

££

❖

NatWest Trophy

Lord's Cricket Ground, St John's Wood Road, NW8 (0171 289 8979: box office)
⊖ St John's Wood
❑ 13, 46, 82, 113, 274
££

Notting Hill Carnival

W11
Every August bank holiday since 1965 Notting Hill has been the scene of London's largest and most popular carnival. Over 100 colourful floats, bands and dancers wind their way through the crowded streets, filling the air with music from South America, Africa, the Caribbean and India, not forgetting the incessant screech of the onlooker's whistles. This heady cocktail of noise and colour is further jazzed up with sound systems sited along the route, producing their own variations of funk, reggae, hip-hop and soul music, while stalls sell exotic foods as well as arts and crafts.

The children's day is usually held on the Sunday, with the main carnival taking place on Monday. A word of warning, though: the area is always extremely busy and provides easy pickings for thieves, so hold on to your money and leave any valuables at home. Parking is difficult, so you are advised to take public transport.
⊖ Notting Hill and Ladbroke Grove are usually closed during the carnival, so use nearby Holland Park or Westbourne Park
❑ 12, 27, 28, 31, 52, 70, 94, 302
Open: early afternoon to early evening for the parades

SEPTEMBER

The Great River Race

More than 150 traditional boats take part in this spectacular and colourful event along the River Thames, from Richmond to Docklands. Viking longboats, Chinese dragonboats and Hawaiian war canoes tend to be some of the more colourful participants. The race starts from below Ham House, Richmond, at 10.00 a.m. and, having passed through central London, usually finishes at Island Gardens, opposite Greenwich Pier, at around 1.00 p.m.
⊖/**BR** Richmond (for start)
DLR Island Gardens (for finish)
❑ 33, H37, 65, 90, 290, 337(for start); D7, D8, D9(for finish)

OCTOBER

Trafalgar Day Service and Parade

Trafalgar Square, WC2
The anniversary of Lord Nelson's great sea victory at the Battle of Trafalgar (21 October 1805) is commemorated annually at 11.00 a.m. at a parade and service by over 500 sea cadets from all over Britain. The public can spectate.
⊖ Charing Cross, Embankment
BR Charing Cross
❑ 3, 6, 9, 11, 12, 13, 15, X15, 23, 24, 29, 53, X53, 77A, 88, 91, 94, 109, 139, 159, 176

Guy Fawkes Night

Guy Fawkes was arrested by Yeomen of the Guard on 5 November 1605, as one of the conspirators in the Gunpowder Plot to blow up King James I and his Parliament. The anniversary of Guy Fawkes's arrest is widely commemorated around London with bonfires and massive firework displays.

For details of firework displays in the London area, contact the London Tourist Board's Fireworks service from mid–October on 01839 123 401. The main, well-established annual displays take place in the following parks and open spaces:

Alexandra Palace, Wood Green, N10
BR Wood Green
❑ W3

Battersea Park, Prince of Wales Drive, SW11
BR Battersea Park
❑ 19, 44, 45A, 49, 137, 137A, 249, 319, 344

Bishop's Park, Fulham Palace Road, SW10
❺ Putney Bridge
❑ 14, 22, 39, 74, 85, 93, 220, 265, 270

Brockwell Park, Dulwich Road, SE24
❺ Brixton
BR Herne Hill, Tulse Hill
❑ 3, 37, 68, 68A, 196

Highbury Fields, off Holloway Road, N7
❺/**BR** Highbury & Islington
❑ 4, 19

Primrose Hill, NW1
BR Chalk Farm
❑ C11, C12, 31

The Lord Mayor's Show

(0171 606 3030: information)

Lord Mayors have played a crucial role in the City of London's history since medieval times. One of the most impressive events in the City's year is the Lord Mayor's Show, which takes place on the second Saturday in November and is the occasion when the newly appointed Lord Mayor traditionally presents himself to his citizens.

Viewing the Lord Mayor's Procession

Important timings along the procession are as follows:
11.00 a.m.   Head of Procession leaves Guildhall by way of
11.15 a.m.   Gresham Street, Prince's Street, Bank Junction
11.30 a.m.   St Paul's Churchyard, south side (at 12.10 p.m. the Lord Mayor is blessed by the Dean and Chapter of St Paul's on the West Front main steps of the Cathedral), Ludgate Hill, Fleet Street
11.50 a.m.   Royal Courts of Justice, The Strand

returning by way of:
1.15 p.m.   Temple Place, Victoria Embankment
1.25 p.m.   Queen Victoria Street (by Blackfriars Bridge)
1.40 p.m.   Guildhall

Opposite: Notting Hill Carnival

The times shown are approximate and refer to the head of the procession. The Lord Mayor's coach passes approximately forty-five minutes after the head of the procession.

⊖ Bank (for start)

❑ 4, 8, 11, 25, 501(for start)

The Lord Mayor's Show

The custom dates back to 1215, when King John gave the citizens of the City of London the special privilege of electing their own Lord Mayor rather than having to accept a royal nominee. The king, however, did insist that each Lord Mayor should present himself to the monarch at Westminster for royal approval. If the king was away, which he often was, the Lord Mayor was to report to the Law Courts, which is what happens today.

The Corporation of London's government is composed of the Lord Mayor, who is elected annually by members of the livery companies (guilds), twenty-five aldermen, who are elected for life, and 153 council members, who are elected annually from twenty-six wards within the City.

The Lord Mayor's coach

❖

Remembrance Sunday

Cenotaph Memorial, Whitehall, SW1

The second Sunday in the month is a memorial day for those in all three Services and Allied Forces who gave their lives in the two world wars and other conflicts. Detachments of the Armed Forces and ex-service men and women assemble at the Cenotaph and band music is played while awaiting the arrival of the Queen at 10.59 a.m.

A two-minute silence at 11.00 a.m. is heralded and ended by a gun fired from Horse Guards Parade, after which the last post is sounded by buglers of the Royal Marines. The Queen then lays a wreath at the Cenotaph, followed by members of the royal family, representatives of the government, Commonwealth governments and the services. The Bishop of London conducts a short service of Remembrance with a blessing, reveille and the national anthem.

Θ Westminster

❏ 3, 11, 12, 24, 53, X53, 77A, 88, 109, 159

Christmas Lights

Christmas lights are switched on daily from dusk to midnight in Bond Street, Jermyn Street, Oxford Street and Regent Street from mid-November. The best known are the Regent Street lights, which are always first switched on by a popular celebrity.

Θ Oxford Circus, Piccadilly Circus

❏ C2, 3, 6, 7, 8, 10, 12, 13, 15, 16A, 23, 25, 53, X53, 55, 73, 88, 94, 98, 113, 135, 137, 137A, 139, 159, 176

DECEMBER

The Christmas Tree and Carol-singing in Trafalgar Square

WC1

Since 1947, the City of Oslo has presented a Norwegian spruce Christmas tree to London as an expression of goodwill and gratitude for Britain's help during the Second World War. The tree is put up in Trafalgar Square in early December and is decorated with white lights. It is lit daily from 3.00 p.m.–midnight until Twelfth Night (6 January).

Carol singing takes place every evening from 8 December to Christmas Eve between 4.00 and 10.00 p.m. in aid of charities.

Θ Charing Cross

❏ 3, 6, 9, 11, 12, 13, 15, X15, 23, 24, 29, 53, X53, 77A, 88, 91, 94, 109, 139, 159, 176

New Year's Eve Celebrations in Trafalgar Square

WC1

Fun and frolics around Nelson's Column, near enough Big Ben to be able to hear it ring in the New Year. Watch out, though: the huge crowd often causes problems.

USEFUL ADDITIONAL INFORMATION

FOR A daily update on outdoor events in London, phone Visitorcall, the London Tourist Board's phone guide.

Simply dial 01839 123 plus the three number shown below for each subject:

Changing the Guard 411
Famous Houses and Gardens 483
Getting around London 430
River Trips 432
Sightseeing Tours and Walks 431
State Opening of Parliament and Trooping the Colour 413
Street Markets 428
Summer in the Park 406
What's on in the Next Three Months 410
Where to Take Children 404

For a weather forecast, phone 01839 500 951.

TOURIST INFORMATION CENTRES RUN BY THE LONDON TOURIST BOARD

Heathrow Terminals 1,2,3
Underground Station Concourse,
Heathrow Airport
Open: 8.00 a.m.– 6.00 p.m.

Selfridges
Oxford Street, W1A 1AB (Basement
Services Arcade)
Open: during store hours

Liverpool Street Underground Station
EC2M 7PN
Open: Monday 8.15 a.m.–7.00 p.m.;
Tuesday–Saturday, 8.30 a.m.– 4.45 p.m.

Victoria Station Forecourt
SW1 5ND
Open: 8.00 a.m.–7.00 p.m.

OTHER TOURIST INFORMATION CENTRES

British Travel Centre

12 Regent Street, SW1Y 4PQ (0181 846 9000)
Open: Monday–Friday, 9.00 a.m.–5.30 p.m.; Saturday and Sunday, 10.00 a.m. – 6.00 p.m.; May–September, Saturday, 9.00 a.m.–5.00 p.m.; personal callers only

Croydon Tourist Information Centre

Katharine Street, Croydon, CR9 1ET (0181 760 5630)
Open: Monday, 9.30 a.m.–7.00 p.m.; Tuesday, 9.30 a.m.–5.00 p.m.; Saturday, 9.00 a.m.–5.00 p.m.

Discover Islington

Visitor Information Centre, 44 Duncan Street, N1 8BL (0171 278 8787)
Open: 9.00 a.m.–5.00 p.m.

Greenwich Tourist Information Centre

46 Greenwich Church Street, SE10 9BL (0181 858 6376)
Open: 11.00 a.m.– 4.30 p.m.

Harrow Tourist Information Centre

Civic Centre, Station Road, Harrow, HA1 2UJ (0181 424 1103)
Open: Monday–Friday, 9.00 a.m.–5.00 p.m.

Hillingdon Tourist Information Centre

Central Library, 14 High Street, Uxbridge, UB8 1HD (01895 250706)
Open: Monday–Friday, 9.30 a.m.–8.00 p.m.; Friday, 9.30 a.m.– 6.00 p.m.; Saturday, 9.30 a.m.– 4.00 p.m.

Hounslow Tourist Information Centre

24 The Treaty Centre, Hounslow High Street, Hounslow, TW3 1ES (0181 572 8279)
Open: Monday and Wednesday, 9.30 a.m. –5.30 p.m.; Tuesday and Saturday, 9.30 a.m.–2.00 p.m.

Lewisham Tourist Information Centre

Lewisham Library, 366 Lewisham High Street, SE13 6LG (0181 690 8325)
Open: Monday and Saturday, 9.30 a.m. –5.30 p.m.; Tuesday and Thursday, 9.30 a.m.–8.00 p.m.; Friday, 9.30 a.m. –1.00 p.m.

London Docklands Development Corporation

Visitors' Centre, 3 Limeharbour, E14 9TJ (0171 512 3000)
Open: 10.00 a.m.–5.00 p.m.

Redbridge Tourist Information Centre

Town Hall, High Road, Ilford, Essex IG1 1DD (0181 478 3020)
Open: Monday–Friday, 8.30 a.m.–5.00 p.m.

Richmond Tourist Information Centre

Old Town Hall, Whittaker Avenue, Richmond, TW9 1TP (0181 940 9125)
Open: Monday–Friday, 10.00 a.m. – 6.00 p.m.; Saturday, 10.00 a.m. –5.00 p.m.; May–October, Sunday, 10.15 a.m.–4.15 p.m.

Twickenham Tourist Information Centre

The Atrium, Civic Centre, York Street, Twickenham, TW1 3BZ (0181 891 7272)
Open: Monday–Friday, 9.00 a.m.–5.15 p.m.

❖

INDEX TO MAPS

WALKERS' LONDON

Index to map on pages 10–11

NATURALISTS' LONDON

Index to map on pages 86–7

SPORTING LONDON

Index to map on pages 124–5

OUTDOOR ENTERTAINMENT

Index to map on pages 150–1

❖

INDEX

AUTHOR'S ACKNOWLEDGEMENTS

Thank you to everyone who helped me with this book. I would particularly like to acknowledge the assistance of the following people and companies: Rebecca Milton and the press office of the London Tourist Board; the information desks of London's borough councils and tourist offices; British Waterways; the Countryside Commission; Common Ground; the Corporation of the City of London; English Heritage; the Garden History Society; the Grand Union Canal Society; Inland Waterways Association; Kew Gardens; the London Docklands Development Corporation; London Regional Transport; London Wildlife Trust; the Natural History Museum; the Ramblers' Association; The Royal Parks Commission; the Royal Society for the Prevention of Cruelty to Animals; the Royal Society for the Protection of Birds; The Sports Council; Thames Water; and finally a big thank-you to Anita Bhambhani for all her help and to Simon and my mother for their encouragement.

PHOTOGRAPH ACKNOWLEDGEMENTS

Photographs courtesy of:
Collections/Robert Hallman 79; **Collections/John Hickman** 122–3; **Collections/Geoff Howard** 13, 16, 19, 39, 57, 72, 136, 159; **Collections/Alain Le Garsmeur** 84–5, 118; **Collections/Keith Pritchard** 55, 77; **Collections/Roger Scruton** 192; **Collections/Brian Shuel** 36, 40, 54, 71, 119, 127, 148–9 183, 187, 196, 198; **Collections/Anthea Sieveking** 103; **Ward Lock** 8–9, 47, 49, 50, 63, 64–5, 66, 67, 152, 157